IN PRAISE OF

FORGING BONDS OF STEEL

"This practical, helpful book gives you precious guidance that can help you to achieve lasting financial success."

BRIAN TRACY

*Professional Speaker, Best Selling Author,
Entrepreneur and Success Expert*

"A brilliant financial advisor is one that not only understands your money, but also truly understand you. How can you build a strong and lasting relationship with this critical partner? Rodger Alan Friedman's spot-on book will show you the way."

SALLY HOGSHEAD

*CEO of How to Fascinate
Author, How the World Sees You*

"With extraordinary clarity, pragmatism, insight, and emotional intelligence, Rodger Friedman masterfully provides a highly useful set of tools and common-sense advice to optimize the all-important relationship with your financial advisor. We've needed a book like this for a long time!"

DAVID M. DARST, CFA

Independent investment consultant, author of 11 books, former Managing Director and Chief Investment Strategist, Morgan Stanley Wealth Management

*"Rodger Friedman's message is timeless.
It's all about the relationship."*

DONALD HECHT, CPA

*Co Founder, Hecht and Company, P.C.
Certified Public Accountants, New York, NY*

"An advisor must put himself at risk with honesty to the client to be effective. Rodger hits the nail on the head about the sacred nature of a client-advisor relationship."

RICHARD WATTS

Author, Fables of Fortune: What Rich People Have that You Don't Want

9/3/2014

FORGING BONDS OF
STEEL

Jonathan,

I am happy to share my
new book with you.

Enjoy!

FORGING BONDS OF

STEEL

HOW TO BUILD A
**SUCCESSFUL AND
LASTING RELATIONSHIP**
WITH YOUR FINANCIAL ADVISOR

RODGER ALAN FRIEDMAN

Published by Advantage, Charleston, South Carolina.
Member of Advantage Media Group.

ADVANTAGE is a registered trademark and the Advantage colophon is a trademark of Advantage Media Group, Inc.

Printed in the United States of America.

ISBN: 978-159932-478-4
LCCN: 2014940535

Book design by George Stevens.

This publication is designed to provide accurate and authoritative information in regard to the subject matter covered. It is sold with the understanding that the publisher is not engaged in rendering legal, accounting, or other professional services. If legal advice or other expert assistance is required, the services of a competent professional person should be sought.

DISCLAIMER: *This information is not intended as a solicitation or an offer to buy or sell any security referred to herein. Keep in mind that there is no assurance that our recommendations or strategies will ultimately be successful or profitable nor protect against a loss. There may also be the potential for missed growth opportunities that may occur after the sale of an investment. Recommendations, specific investments or strategies discussed may not be suitable for all investors. Past performance may not be indicative of future results. You should discuss any tax or legal matters with the appropriate professional.*

Advantage Media Group is proud to be a part of the Tree Neutral® program. Tree Neutral offsets the number of trees consumed in the production and printing of this book by taking proactive steps such as planting trees in direct proportion to the number of trees used to print books. To learn more about Tree Neutral, please visit **www.treeneutral.com**. To learn more about Advantage's commitment to being a responsible steward of the environment, please visit **www.advantagefamily.com/green**

For more insight from the mind of Rodger Friedman, visit

FORGINGBONDSOFSTEEL.COM

ACKNOWLEDGMENTS

I would like to thank all of the wonderful people at Advantage Media Group whose guidance made this book possible. First and foremost, I thank Alison Morse, Advantage's very own Wonder Woman, who helped me to get to the starting line. I am grateful for her encouragement and wealth of knowledge. I also thank Brooke White, who helped me make great choices; Jenn Ash, for her assistance as I asked silly questions while trying to make good decisions; George Stevens, whose tireless efforts in the final design of this book made me shout with joy; Bob Sheasley, who spent countless hours consulting with me in the editing of this book; and Denis Boyles, who provided guidance from on high.

Last, but certainly not least, I thank Adam Witty, CEO of Advantage, who took the time to chat with an author wannabe at a conference in Florida. This book became a reality because I purchased a riveting book for a Cape Cod vacation that also contained an offer to join an entrepreneurial organization. After reading eight other Dan S. Kennedy books and countless newsletters, I booked a spot at a super-conference in Orlando, where I chatted with Adam. The rest, as they say, is history.

IN MEMORY

Many experienced investment advisors continue to work with the families of long-time clients who have passed away. This is an emotionally difficult time when estate issues need to be settled in a caring and supportive manner.

In my practice, I have been fortunate to work with many beneficiaries whose assets were originally entrusted to my care by someone who was close to them and who died. I strive to keep earning their trust and confidence each day.

For this reason, this book is dedicated to the 36 wonderful clients, friends, and family members whom I have served and who have passed away during the more than three decades that I have practiced:

Andy F.	Joan R.	Dick V.	Vivian F.
Rose F.	David M.	Herb Z.	Howard F.
Bill E.	Marie M.	Bernard C.	Marguerite G.
Tom E.	Ruth H.	George R.	Kathy P.
Mike R.	Helen D.	Genieve R.	Hazel M.
Mike B.	Evelyn S.	Nick B.	Mary K.
Michael H.	Myra S.	Lois B.	Robert F.
Dottie H.	Joann M.	Walter V.	Paul N.
Dolores H.	Frank M.	Joe J.	Mary V.

TABLE OF CONTENTS

ABOUT THE AUTHOR

Rodger Alan Friedman grew up in the 1960s in Manhattan's Lower East Side, the youngest in a family of five. His father owned and managed the family laundry that was started by his grandparents. Rodger is a product of the New York City public school system (but you should not hold that against him). He divided his time among riding his bicycle, reading comic books, playing ball, doing homework, riding his skateboard, and watching TV. Rodger takes great pride in the fact that famous people attended Seward Park, his high school on Delancey Street on the Lower East Side. Although Rodger never attended classes with Walter Matthau, Tony Curtis, or Zero Mostel, he loves to say they went to "his school."

After school, for many summers, Rodger worked in the family laundry. It was there that he learned about capitalism and the work he *did not want* to pursue as an adult. As a political science major at a small, public, upstate New York college, Rodger also learned that he had little respect for politics and less for politicians.

Rodger's upbringing was "entrepreneurial middle class." Dinner conversation always included classwork, lectures on acceptable behavior, the problems at the laundry, and the movement of the Dow Jones Industrial Average. Rodger felt the gentle push to figure out his path in the world. His elder brother, Bruce, was an electrical engineer and his sister, Donna, a social worker. Surely, the universe had something more interesting than dirty laundry in mind for him.

Rodger's childhood ways were cut short by the death of his mother, shortly before he turned 13 years of age. Soon, he was the one making shopping trips to the grocery and attending to other chores that were never part of his earlier life. He found he needed to grow up faster than he had intended.

After graduating from college and moving to Queens with his college roommate, he landed his first non-laundry-related job. He found his six months as a trainee real-estate agent to be less than inspiring. He spent his days surveying midtown Manhattan office space and learning which hotels had the coldest air-conditioning and fanciest rest rooms.

Fate drew him to the *New York Times* classified ads, and he found himself a new career on Wall Street. Rodger took great interest in the securities industry and became part of a team that performed compliance audits for branch offices of E.F. Hutton across the nation. His work involved the rules and regulations of the firm and government agencies.

After spending two years questioning and reviewing the stockbrokers in scores of branch offices, Rodger moved to Washington, DC, and became operations manager of a large branch of E.F. Hutton & Co. After two years, he lost interest in the sameness of the issues he faced daily and applied for the stockbroker-training program. It was in the fall of 1984 that Rodger became a stockbroker with E.F. Hutton.

Over the next three decades, Rodger grew his skills, knowledge, experience, and practice, and today he continues to feel passionate about what he is doing: focusing on advising affluent retirees and near-retirees in structuring their planning and investments for the next phase of their lives. He lives in Rockville, Maryland, with his wife, Reena, and their children, Avery and Jason.

If you wish to contact Rodger Friedman, e-mail him at Rodger@ForgingBondsofSteel.com, or by simply searching on the web for his name in the Washington, D.C. metropolitan area. He serves as a wealth manager, managing director and founding partner of Steward Partners Global Advisory.

AUTHOR'S NOTE

I have attempted to bring some of the lessons in this book alive through the use of storytelling. I have blended elements from many client experiences to make a point. I have been careful to change names, places, and circumstances to safeguard identities, and any similarity to actual client events may be minimal at best. Should you find a story that has any similarity to your own life, you are permitted a smile, but only a brief one.

₧

MADE TO ENDURE

"WEALTH IS THE PRODUCT OF MAN'S CAPACITY TO THINK."

AYN RAND

I held my grandfather's hand and waved as my parents boarded the ship for a cruise leaving New York harbor. I marveled at the heavy chains that held the transatlantic ocean liner securely to the pier and watched in wonder as those chains retreated into the hold, each link the size of a suitcase. To an eight-year-old, they seemed magnificent in their ability to restrain so many tons of power.

I can close my eyes today and still see those massive steel links forged for the purpose of keeping a ship safe for its next journey. As a financial advisor, I like to think of my relationship with my clients that way: as bonds of steel that endure for the long haul.

As a financial advisor, I like to think of my relationship with my clients that way: as bonds of steel that endure for the long haul.

I drifted into that sort of reverie one recent December as I sat by my fireplace, reading *Atlas Shrugged* for the fourteenth time. It was snowing, but I was toasty in my home. I had gotten into the habit of re-reading my favorite book during the holiday season each year. For two weeks each December, I have been swept away in this 1,100-page epic novel that I have come to love.

I was reading Ayn Rand's description of the foundry at the Rearden mills in Pennsylvania, where molten steel is poured from the great furnace. And it occurred to me that I have forged scores of relationships with my clients. They are bonds as strong as those steel chains on an ocean liner. I think Ayn Rand might approve.

I did not write this book to give you investment advice. If that's what you are looking for, close it now and put it back on the shelf. There are hundreds of books in the marketplace that do that. I would have nothing to add to what's already been written. Do you actually need another book on municipal bonds or dividend income investing? There are many places where you could find advice—books, magazines, the Internet, or your brother-in-law.

Investment advice is everywhere. It has become a commodity. What has not become a commodity is the personal relationship between you and your advisor. That cannot be replaced by the web or an iPhone app.

My purpose in writing this book is to help you understand the elements that make up a truly beneficial advisory relationship. Call it the human element. My hope is that

For two weeks each December, I have been swept away in this 1,100-page epic novel that I have come to love.

you will come away with some tools, strategies, and distinctions to help you strengthen the bond between you and your financial advisor. My goal is that you have an effective and successful relationship with that person or team.

YOU NEED TRUST, NOT THEORIES

There are no lengthy departures into theory in these pages. What you will read is distilled from my first-hand observations and experience as a participant in the retail brokerage and wealth management industry. I will discuss what works and what doesn't. We will talk about trust and why your advisor needs to be relevant in your life. I will share with you examples and lessons that I have learned. Perhaps you will draw some parallels with your own advisor and your own experiences.

INVESTMENT ADVICE IS EVERYWHERE. IT HAS BECOME A COMMODITY. WHAT HAS NOT BECOME A COMMODITY IS THE PERSONAL RELATIONSHIP BETWEEN YOU AND YOUR ADVISOR.

I have met many talented and knowledgeable people in the industry. I clearly remember what I was told when I was hired by E.F. Hutton, "There are many very smart people here, and if you hang around long enough, you'll get it." I spent the better part of 34 years at that firm, even as it changed its name more than a few times.

When I started my career in 1980, the world was very different. For one thing, I had a full head of black hair. Not so today. That was the year that Ronald Reagan took office as president. The cost of a first-class postage stamp was 15 cents, and John Lennon was shot dead on the streets of my hometown. I was 24 years old.

I spend my days advising clients. People who do what I do are known by many names: financial consultant, wealth management advisor, investment advisor, account executive, financial planner, investment executive, and financial advisor. In this book, I use the terms *consultant, advisor,* and *planner* interchangeably. Regardless of the label, the best of the best share many common characteristics in how they forge bonds of trust with the families they serve. Good advisors are acutely aware that to build and sustain a genuine relationship with a client, their message must reflect both authenticity and sincerity.

A trusting relationship with your financial advisor is worth its weight in gold. Sharing personal and closely held issues might feel uncomfortable at times, but without openness between you and your advisor, what do you think you will really accomplish? Would your doctor be able to solve your health challenges if you did not tell him your symptoms or where it hurt?

It's up to you to determine how much time and effort you will put into your relationship with your advisor. You get out what you put in. Perhaps you take a week to return your advisor's call, if you return it at all. Or perhaps you always call back as soon as you can. It bewilders me when an advisor says a client doesn't return calls on an important issue. Is it more important to the advisor than to the client? We will discuss this in length in the pages to come.

Years ago, a great friend and college roommate of mine, Stu Schnirman, said that life becomes easier when you know someone has your back. I'm sure he would see the value of an engaged, attentive, and seasoned financial advisor monitoring your assets as someone having your back. I've been advising families on their finances and investments for three decades. I have witnessed patterns of success and failure—and I too have experienced both in my life. The personal development speaker Brian Tracy, my mentor, taught me that success lies on the far side of failure. You cannot expect to succeed if you haven't experienced failure at some point.

As I was considering this book, I thought of the many instances when I developed strong bonds with clients and those times when I failed to make that connection. It is far easier to write about that dynamic than to consistently get it right. I consider myself a work in progress.

One day I listed, page after page, the characteristics of my best client relationships, those clients I had lost, and the prospects I had never convinced to become clients. It wasn't a matter of showing people how much I knew. What I most likely had failed to demonstrate was that I would care enough, that I could be trusted to be a steward of their assets, and that I had the resources, knowledge, and experience to be an effective partner. I was told a long time ago that clients must be absolutely convinced that the advisor cares more about them than anyone else, except those who share their last name.

ONE LINK AT A TIME

Forging trust, like links in a chain, requires time. Trust evolves and strengthens. For example, I have been working side by side with my business partner, Joe Wong, for six years, and my wife, Reena, knows that if I were to pass away tomorrow, Joe would be my first and best choice to manage our funds in my absence. As a Certified Financial Planner® and Chartered Retirement Plans Specialist, he would ensure prudent practices with the necessary knowledge, trustworthiness, and experience. He has shown a commitment to personal development and intellectual challenge. He has a love of knowledge and is one of the most ethical people I have ever met. I consider myself blessed that we are a team.

The trust I have for Joe evolved over time. It did not appear the day I met him. It was forged one link at a time, one interaction after another. Time after time, I watched as he always placed clients' interests first and went the extra mile, significantly exceeding our clients' expectations. I believe that Joe's parents instilled his ethics deeply.

In my financial services career, as I served in legal and compliance and branch operations departments, as well as advising clients directly, I have read and seen what happens when advisor–client relationships end poorly. The outcomes are characterized by anger, financial losses, arbitration, job termination, or litigation. From time to time I have witnessed what happens when trust breaks down in an advisor–client relationship, if it was ever there. Accusations fly and tempers come to a boil as management and lawyers get involved. I would wager that in these instances, the clients' needs were not placed first, nor was there open, honest, and frequent communication.

A bond of trust between the advisor and client might have prevented such hardships. This is the lesson: make sure your relationship is sufficiently strong and enduring that you will be confident that your advisor always places your interests first.

MAKE SURE YOUR RELATIONSHIP IS SUFFICIENTLY STRONG AND ENDURING THAT YOU WILL BE CONFIDENT THAT YOUR ADVISOR ALWAYS PLACES YOUR INTERESTS FIRST.

"We're wired to attach our own security and safety to the idea of trust, so when those bonds are broken, we feel threatened," Sally Hogshead wrote in *Fascinate: Your 7 Triggers to Persuasion and Captivation*. "Broken trust can have disastrous effects, requiring serious effort, time, and a savvy plan to rebuild."

ꝏ

"I NEVER THOUGHT OF THAT!"

"I FINALLY KNOW WHAT DISTINGUISHES MAN FROM OTHER BEASTS: FINANCIAL WORRIES."

JULES RENARD

I learned a lot about life on West 45th Street in New York City. That was the home of Norton's Laundry and Dry Cleaning Company, my dad's store near Times Square.

As the owner's kid, I got to do all of the dirty work that would later be described as character building. Working behind a dry cleaning machine in the summer, at 105 degrees, is a rather strange breeding ground for work on Wall Street. I did get out for a bit of fresh air each day, walking all around Times Square with 40 pounds of dry cleaning garments on hangers slung over my shoulders.

I often wanted to leave early to be with my friends, perhaps take in a movie at the Academy of Music on 14th Street, hang out in Greenwich Village, or play ball in Stuyvesant Town, where we lived.

But my father, Andy Friedman, would have none of it. The work was not done until he said it was done. He could bring a smile to a drill sergeant's face. More than once, he threatened to rip the clock off the wall when he saw that I was paying more attention to it than to the task at hand. "The clock does not tell you when you are done," he would say. "When the work is completed correctly, that's when you are done. Stop looking at the clock and get back to work."

I loved my dad. I just did not like the work I was assigned to do. I always preferred to wait on the customers at the front counter and use the cash register. I got to work with two things I enjoyed: people and their money.

Though I didn't enjoy much of the labor, I did understand the importance of what I did and how it related to what other employees were doing. *I was part of a process*, and my part had to be completed before others could do their part. Our store was not small. My dad had three dozen employees at Norton's Laundry. They were trying to earn a living, to bring home money for their families. I was just trying to earn extra money for a bicycle, comic books, pizza, and a movie.

LEARNING TO DO IT RIGHT

I started to see that it really didn't matter whether I liked the work. It had to be done. Over time, that sunk in. As I drove the laundry truck, I saw how important it was to people all over the city, waiting for their clean, pressed shirts, or to the performers down the block at the Broadway Theater, waiting for their clean costumes.

It wasn't brain surgery, nor was I fending off a Communist threat, but it was important to my dad, so it became important to me. I saw the importance of making sure everything that needed to be done was completed before we closed up the store and went home for the evening. I remember the feeling, as I shut and locked the heavy steel gates during a winter snowstorm, that I was protecting our livelihood. *A work ethic was born at that store.*

I can see now that the family work ethic went back much further. My dad inherited it from his mom and dad, my grandpa, Max and grandma, Rose. My grandmother was born in 1911 in a small Russian town outside Minsk. Her father owned a general store. All of the children worked in the store, which, it seems, is a trait that runs in the family. It was hard work. It had to be done. It was what enabled the family to survive. My grandma told me that no one in the community really worked for anyone else. There were no companies. You made shoes or you butchered cows or you made candles or furniture. That was what you did.

I remember the feeling, as I shut and locked the heavy steel gates during a winter snowstorm, that I was protecting our livelihood. A work ethic was born at that store.

My grandmother was very stern when I was working for her at Norton's Laundry. My first job was putting on hanger guards for a penny each. The guard prevents pants from creasing on the hanger. After doing 300 or 400, I wanted to quit, but my grandmother would show me the 20 or 30 that didn't look right and had to be done again. She told me it had to be done right or not at all. I loved my Grandma Rose, but as Mrs. Norton with a thick Russian accent, she was a no-nonsense boss.

A MODEL FOR PROSPERITY

My dad had a respectable operation going. We had three trucks, making deliveries all over the city, and I watched how he directed everything. I observed how he prospered over time. Our Oldsmobile was replaced by a Cadillac. I was only allowed in the back seat. His rule was that no one but an adult would drive that car.

I think back now and remember watching how hard my dad worked for the money he earned. In my mind, something clicked. Hard work and earning a superior income went hand in hand. Evidently, I was learning as I sweated in the back of the store, folding hundreds of draperies. Perhaps, that is what my dad had in mind after all.

I saw over time that his work ethic was the core of his life. It didn't matter that he didn't want to get out of bed at 5:30 a.m. and get to the store. It had to be done. There were many employees arriving at the store. If they couldn't work, everything would grind to a halt.

I learned that successful people do what unsuccessful people are unwilling to do. I despised waking up at "o'dark thirty" (still dark outside) and going to work with him. But I learned from watching him what you needed to do to be successful.

He was good at getting things done, at organizing, and at planning. As I watched him do this, day after day, year after year, it sank in. I felt that these were characteristics to develop in whatever business I went into. I am amazed today at how disorganized people can be—even financial advisors. Make sure your advisor is organized. If you see stacks of unfiled papers, yours might be among them. If you can't see the wood on the desktop, run!

Some of my tasks at the laundry were fun, such as using a steam gun to remove stains on clothing. I liked to imagine I was shooting a gun in a Western shootout. But if my dad saw me doing such things, he would scold me and tell me to first do the important tasks he had assigned me. The easy tasks and the fun could wait.

I hated doing the hard stuff, such as pinning draperies to be hung in homes and office buildings. Putting in pins to hang up drapes does not sound like a bad job, until you see hundreds of draperies waiting, with 50 pins each. Worse yet was when I had to take the pins out of filthy drapes that came in to be cleaned. My hands ached, and dust and dirt flew in the air and all over my face.

I learned every job in the place with one exception. I never could learn how to accurately measure a new drapery installation job. I got it wrong each and every time I tried. I learned to live with that failure, and I moved on.

As much as I detested doing the dirty work in the laundry, I smile a knowing smile, because my work ethic was born there. Without that work ethic, I would not have accomplished what I have accomplished. Through the years working for my dad, I watched, I listened, and I learned. Maybe he knew it. Maybe he didn't, but he was a great teacher.

AS MUCH AS I DETESTED DOING THE DIRTY WORK IN
THE LAUNDRY, MY WORK ETHIC WAS BORN THERE.

I would watch my dad near the end of the workday, with his yellow legal pad and pencil. Each and every evening, he wrote down what he had to accomplish the next day and put a star next to the most important items. My father's pad and pencil allowed him to be both efficient and effective in running his business. He was methodical about doing the most important things first. He was an expert in time management before anyone knew what time management was.

I have replaced my dad's yellow pad with a spiral notebook. If he were alive today, I don't think he would mind the upgrade. I hear that even Donald Trump keeps a spiral notebook on his desk at Trump Tower.

EXPANDING HORIZONS

From my home on the Lower East Side, I could walk to the United Nations, Times Square, the Empire State Building, or Greenwich Village. It was as if the world were a stroll away, and my horizons eventually expanded a little further when I went to college upstate near Rochester, where it was very cold. As an undergraduate, I pursued a political science degree.

In 1980 I started work for E.F. Hutton, doing internal compliance audits and traveling nationwide to dozens and dozens of branches, interviewing operations personnel and their stockbrokers. Over time, in questioning hundreds of advisors, I came to understand what makes up a good one and what makes up a bad one.

As I was doing my audits, I always came back to the idea that I'd like to return to Washington, DC, one day. I had spent a semester there in college and enjoyed the city. It was like a smaller, cleaner version of New York. I told myself that if I ever had the chance, I would go back.

After about two years in the internal audit department, I got my chance when the manager of a Washington branch was looking for a new operations manager. I got the position and was overjoyed that I would be pursuing my career there. After two years in that position, I went into the E.F. Hutton training program and became a stockbroker in 1984.

My career has evolved over the years. In the 1980s, it was very common to have a stockbroker but not a financial advisor. As I have taken numerous courses, read many books, and attended workshops and lectures, I have gone beyond the scope of the stockbroker I once was. I have, typically, worked 60 hours a week for the last 30 years. Back-of-the-envelope math tells me I have about 90,000 hours of experience in doing what I do.

I HAVE, TYPICALLY, WORKED 60 HOURS A WEEK FOR THE LAST 30 YEARS. BACK-OF-THE-ENVELOPE MATH TELLS ME I HAVE ABOUT 90,000 HOURS OF EXPERIENCE IN DOING WHAT I DO.

RETIRING WITH CONFIDENCE

Today I lead an investment team at a Washington-based wealth-management firm. The focus of the team is to advise and coach middle-class millionaires in developing retirement income strategies so that they can enjoy their retirement with confidence.

Our clients do not own yachts or jets, nor do they have limousines with chauffeurs. They are people who have amassed their wealth a couple of thousand bucks at a time over and over, decade by decade. They do not think of themselves as rich.

They have an affluent state of mind but are mindful of all the years it took to reach their state of wealth. Many of these people think of themselves as middle class, even if their net worth is \$3 or \$4 million. The idea of a \$4,500-per-month mortgage would make them cringe.

There are no tech geniuses among them, nor any dot-com millionaires, just professors, plumbers, doctors, lawyers, corporate senior managers, store owners, and military retirees. We serve widows and widowers, and many, many grandparents. I generally work with individuals who have less than \$10 million of investable assets.

They are, basically, family people. They are people who saved for their kids' college education month by month. They are people concerned about where their retirement income will come from and how to make that income more predictable. They want to know that they will have a retirement paycheck each month. There may be seven figures in their net worth, but they are exceedingly middle class in their *emotional relationship with money.*

A RELATIONSHIP OF CARING

At its heart, this book is primarily about relationships. When a financial advisor and a client get to know each other, they become involved in each other's lives. They talk about more than the investment portfolio or the IRA account. They talk about each other's children and the concerns that parents share. They talk about setting aside money for a grandchild's education. They talk about increasing cash flow to allow for more gifting. They discuss whether the income from a municipal bond is really free of federal income tax. They talk about all these things, and they talk about life.

I try to be an important part of the lives of our clients. I have been to weddings, memorial services, funerals, and bar mitzvahs. I've been to family gatherings, not as one of the family but as a close family associate. I meet many of their relatives.

I have found that level of personal caring deepens the quality of the professional caring. The relationship assumes greater depth and richness. Your advisor feels free to offer— and you are grateful to accept—more than gentle encouragement. You may get a loud warning. Every once in a while, people who do what I do have to beat their chests and shout from the highest tree, "Don't do that!"

I HAVE FOUND THAT LEVEL OF PERSONAL CARING DEEPENS THE QUALITY OF THE PROFESSIONAL CARING. THE RELATIONSHIP ASSUMES GREATER DEPTH AND RICHNESS.

Nick Murray is one of the wisest people I have ever met. He is an author and teacher who specializes in my industry. Like me, he was an account executive, or stockbroker, at E.F. Hutton decades ago. I have read his books, attended his lectures, and taken notes. He often retells the story of saying, "Don't do that!" to a client.

I am grateful to now have that in my own tool chest.

That's what great advisors often say to clients when they tell us that family, friends, or other advisors have asked them for investment money. Picture this: You are widowed with a pension, Social Security, and a moderate investment portfolio that provides reasonable income. One of your advisors hawks an investment opportunity in a start-up business with a buy-in of $50,000, or even $100,000. You don't know what to think. It seems like a good idea, but you're not sure. You call someone who does what I do to provide a second opinion, to give you some confidence.

I remember hearing a story told to me at a seminar where an advisor never got the buy-in from the client because another advisor stood up and shouted, "Don't do that." That story ended with the investment opportunity going bankrupt. All investor funds were lost. The client continues to receive her income from a rationally diversified portfolio that is designed to focus on income with a reasonable opportunity for growth.

As an investor, one of the best feelings you can have is when your advisor is acting as a steward of your portfolio and guardian of your assets. Granted, it's not as if Superman is standing guard over your account, but it sure beats being out in the cold with no one watching your back.

Many of my clients can attest to the fact that, at some point in our relationship, I asked their permission to be a nudge. The definition is "to push slightly or gently, especially with the elbow, to get someone's attention or to prod someone to action." It's a role that a good advisor will play and a good client will accept. It's a relationship to treasure. It means someone is looking out for you.

MANY OF MY CLIENTS CAN ATTEST TO THE FACT THAT, AT SOME POINT IN OUR RELATIONSHIP, I ASKED THEIR PERMISSION TO BE A NUDGE.

FACING THE MUSIC

Jack and Diane lived in a split level home on the outskirts of Washington, DC. Diane worked part-time at a local college admissions office, and Jack was the manager of a plumbing supply house. Between their jobs, they had almost $115,000 in annual income. They were not extravagant in their spending but had a beautiful home, a reasonably sized mortgage, and each drove moderately priced, dependable cars.

They paid their credit card bills in full at the end of each month. They had twin daughters who just turned 12.

The girls loved gymnastics and were really good at it. Jack and Diane took turns taking the girls to gymnastic practices four days a week. It was two months after their daughters' birthday when Diane and Jack met their advisor for a comprehensive review of their finances.

He learned that Diane had grown up in the South, one of six sisters, and had a love of growing vegetables in her own garden and trying out the old family recipes passed on from her great-grandmother. Diane would make wonderful soups and stews, using what she grew in her garden behind her home. Both Diane and her daughters worked the garden. Jack used to belong to a jazz band when he was growing up in Atlanta. He was an only son with a long line of history buffs in his family, dating back over 100 years. His enjoyment of history was tied to this love of music, which continued into his married years. He was an avid collector of 1940s and 1950s jazz records from the great masters of horn, saxophone, and trumpet. His record collection, long-playing 33-rpm albums, was extensive and worth a small fortune. He took great pride in showing them off. Jack once took his advisor to the famous Blues Alley Jazz Club in Washington to see and hear Stanley Turrentine play his saxophone. He was trans-fixed by his musical genius and became a lifelong fan.

As they reviewed the raw data that was to be used to construct their financial plan, their advisor stopped cold when he reached the section dealing with life insurance coverage. Their coverage was not at all adequate for their family. They believed it was sufficient for their needs, and they moved on to the next section of the financial questionnaire. Their advisor stopped the conversation and began writing down some simple math on a yellow legal pad. They watched as he wrote numbers in columns, did some calculations, and turned the pad around so they could read it.

He showed them that with their savings, investments, and insurance coverage, if Jack were to pass away suddenly, the family would have no more than a modest annual income, a far cry from their current income of almost $115,000. To say the least, they were shocked. They did not understand how the very reasonable choices that they thought they had made were so wrong. In the coming weeks, they created a strategy that combined additional group coverage from his employer, as well as individually owned insurance.

Jack saw that the plan they drew up was reasonable and well suited to the family's needs. The only problem he saw was that there would be no extra money left to pursue his passion for collecting those rare recordings of the jazz greats. Jack looked at the paperwork, looked at Diane, and signed all of the needed documents on the spot. He told his wife that she and their daughters were most important in his life, and his jazz collection could wait. Their advisor congratulated them on making a prudent decision. He knew it was the right thing to do.

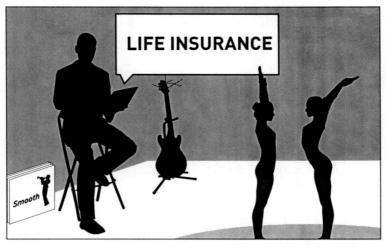

Jack told his wife that she and their daughters were most important in his life, and his jazz collection could wait.

Four years later, as Jack drove home through a storm, his car was hit by a tractor trailer on the Washington beltway. Jack died instantly from a massive head trauma. A well-designed insurance program would provide the needed funds for Diane and her girls to continue on and stay in their home. Today both girls attend college with the funds that were made available from the life insurance program. Diane still tends her garden, works part time at the college, and plays the music her husband loved so much.

Financial advisors are aware each and every day that our actions, or inactions, affect lives in a very real and meaningful way. If your advisor points out a problem with your planning, listen closely and determine if you feel the same after you have all the facts. ○

WE CONTROL ONLY OUR BEHAVIOR

Your advisor must be focused on the continuous and deliberate improvement of your financial circumstances. When I began my career, I was under the mistaken impression that my job was to manage assets. I have learned that my job was also to manage expectations and behavior.

Years ago, I would involve myself with the technical aspect of portfolio construction, only to lose sight of my clients' motivations and unspoken objectives. My mistake was that I did not take the time to understand my clients' deepest feelings about what the funds meant to them and their goals for the future. My expectations for the accounts were not in sync with theirs, and that produced a disconnect.

Since then, I have strived to understand my clients' beliefs, values and their motivations so that we agree about which actions would help or hurt their progress and management of assets.

Those who have a trusted relationship with their advisors are confident that they could rely on them to do what they say they will do, when they say they will do it. This happens over time. As you have positive experiences, you create the expectation that they will continue, and you build trust even further. You are forging those links.

I have had numerous discussions with financial advisors from many firms who tell me how they cope with all of the uncertainties involved in wealth management. So many variables are outside their control, such as the direction of interest rates, Federal Reserve Bank policy, the stock market, and tax law changes.

However, they emphasize that the one and only thing in life that they can control is their own behavior. It is behavior, not talk, that reveals personal responsibility, says business consultant Dan S. Kennedy. Regardless of market gyrations, near-zero interest rates, and political gridlock, good financial advisors work to make a difference in the lives of their clients.

I consider the author Jim Rohn to be another of my mentors, though I never met him. I have listened to his recorded seminars, for several years, in my car, while commuting. Rohn was a genius of a business philosopher. "What happens, happens to us all," he was known to tell his audiences. "It is how we respond that makes all the difference."

BRINGING IDEAS TO THE TABLE

I'm gratified when I hear clients say, "I never thought of that." That means I unearthed what was important to them and gave them an idea that they could act upon and that could benefit them and their family. I see that as value added. We might give a client the idea to:

- Fund his son's Roth IRA with monthly contributions while his son saves for a house and pays for college classes.

- Become a savvy college savings plan investor for their four grandchildren. Not long ago, they had never even heard the term college savings plan.

- Collaborate with their estate-planning attorney in completing legacy plans with provisions to protect their children's inheritance from possible divorces or lawsuits.

- Become more educated regarding the mortgage on her beachfront property, setting up a conference call with a mortgage company and the client's CPA.

℞ Become grateful that their financial plan shows they will have the cash flow in retirement to live as they choose and that they can assist their daughter in ways they did not think possible.

A highlight of what I do is presenting ideas that clients had not considered. In my experience, I've learned a thing or two about what works and what doesn't work. Success leaves clues, as life coach Tony Robbins says. I have seen where I have messed up. I have seen where I have succeeded. I understand that the path to success is narrow and that one must be careful to stay on it.

PRUDENT JUDGMENT

In Ayn Rand's *Atlas Shrugged* a reporter asks railroad executive Dagney Taggert how she knows that a bridge made of a new kind of metal will support a train with 80 loaded freight cars weighing thousands of tons. Her answer was telling: What was going to support it was *her judgment.*

And that's why you commit to a relationship with a financial advisor. You are engaging with someone whose experience and capacity for reasoned analysis has matured to prudent judgment. That judgment is often based upon thousands of hours of experience in working with people with issues much like yours.

Knowledge and judgment are not the same. I have met many knowledgeable simpletons. They are like parrots. Their knowledge does not impress me. I feel annoyed by the incessant spouting of useless facts. They lack judgment.

KNOWLEDGE AND JUDGMENT ARE NOT THE SAME. I HAVE MET MANY KNOWLEDGEABLE SIMPLETONS. THEY ARE LIKE PARROTS.

Think of the matters in your own life in which you believe you have good judgment. Did it appear overnight? Or is sound judgment learned through experience as one encounters situations over and over again?

It is not enough for financial advisors to know a lot of investment information. Without the experience to organize that knowledge into useful advice, all of the information is wasted. Ideally, your advisor is not the kind who makes promises or gives guarantees but instead will listen, guide, and assist you toward your goals.

SIZE OF BOOKSHELF VERSUS SIZE OF TV

If you agree that experience is gained by doing something hundreds or thousands of times, you will want an advisor with such a background. I have worked alongside advisors who have finely honed their craft. It is a pleasure to watch them interact with clients.

In the mid-1980s, when I was a newly minted stockbroker for E.F. Hutton in Washington, I had the opportunity to witness one of the most knowledgeable and successful advisors at work. His name has become legendary in our industry, and I will not disclose it here. I had done enough things correctly to land an appointment with a rather large corporate prospect. At the time, it was the rule that junior brokers teamed up with experienced advisors, so I reached out to this superstar.

He was only too happy to help a new broker, and we agreed to work the case together. On the day of the appointment, we walked in side by side, yellow legal pads in hand. I sat amazed for the next hour as my partner asked all of the right questions, dug deep, and listened to the company owner to understand the real motivations.

He took precise notes. He didn't even have a script. His knowledge of pension investing, asset allocation, and what the prospect was really worried about as a trustee of his pension plan was, to me, quite remarkable. I dreamed of being able to someday do what he did.

In subsequent meetings with my partner and this prospect, I had a front-row seat to watch a confident and knowledgeable professional at work. We, or I should say he, landed the business, a multimillion dollar pension account. He was responsible for all of the important work while I, basically, watched and handled endless details.

Although he tried hard to include me in all aspects of the closing process, I recognized that I was just along for the ride, taking notes and watching excellence in action. I wanted to be like him. I wanted his knowledge and experience, his humble way of getting a point across. I wanted to learn to tie my tie as he did. I even wanted his shoes.

I asked him what I needed to do to one day be as good as he was. He smiled and looked me in the eye. He told me I had to read a lot, as he did. He gave me a list of 12 books to get started. He told me to read about our industry for an hour a day, seven days a week, consistently. He said that 80 percent of the competition didn't bother doing that, but it was a wonderful way to march to the top of the profession. He told me the competing brokers seemed to have time for happy hour but not for reading a book.

I got the message, and I took it seriously. It was one of the most important life lessons I have ever learned, right up there with the lessons from my dad.

To this day, when I visit people's homes, I make a mental note of the size of their bookshelf versus the size of their television. It says a lot about which is more important to them. ◯

THE POWER OF BOOKS

Seriously: Would you trust an advisor who does not read? While I greatly value the experience that comes from dealing with situations over and over again and attending conferences and workshops, in my heart I also value the knowledge that comes from reading books. You may learn something from a magazine article, a TV show, or a webinar, but I would not want that information as a steady diet to gain knowledge.

I would want to know that an advisor reads books on the best thinking in wealth management, economics, investment, and retirement planning. Ideally, your advisor would also attend, participate, and learn from others at seminars. In other words, good advisors are engaged and continually learning, not resting on what they learned 10 years ago.

Would you continue to use a doctor who had not kept up with important research and medical advances since graduating from medical school? I don't think so. It is paramount that doctors continually expand their knowledge. For this reason, I have made it a habit to read a book each week, to listen to experts teach courses on CDs while driving in my car, and to attend workshops that continually allow me to expand my knowledge and abilities.

WOULD YOU CONTINUE TO USE A DOCTOR
WHO HAD NOT KEPT UP WITH IMPORTANT
RESEARCH AND MEDICAL ADVANCES?

From time to time during my career, I have been asked to speak with new financial advisors after they have completed their training in far off places such as New York, New Jersey, or Connecticut. They plant themselves in an office with all of their tests passed and their licenses out for all to see. We talk about how they plan to market themselves and gain clients, and which specialties they wish to focus on, such as college funding, municipal tax-free bonds, or corporate retirement plans. We discuss how they will increase their knowledge so that they become increasingly valuable to their clients.

Many are less than enthusiastic when I suggest a reading list of books. Some tell me they are exhausted from all of the reading and testing they did at school and want to get away from it for a while. When I hear that, I am reminded that a large percentage of Americans do not read books after graduating from school. I consider that a shame.

A CONVERSATION STARTER

I stared out my office window into a rainy February night in Washington. Ten floors below me, long lines of taillights inched along the street. As I watched them, I wondered how I could serve a greater audience than just my clients.

My eyes traveled from the street to my bookshelf, on which I have dozens of books by some of the brightest and most articulate authors in the financial services arena. I have read them all. Each one is geared to the advisor. They were all written for people like me on how to work effectively with clients.

I stared out of my office window into a rainy February night in Washington. I wondered how I could serve a greater audience than just my clients.

Those authors had gotten their stories out, but my own story was still locked inside me. I was not an author, and I couldn't see how I would become one. "I am a financial advisor, not a writer," I said to myself, and then I thought of my dad. He drummed into me at an early age that successful people use the *how* word, not the *can't* word.

How? How indeed? How might I become an author and write a book on creating and improving people's relationships with their financial advisors?

I have long felt that I had a book inside me, but I never knew when it was going to come out. I wrote short stories in college and kept journals. I'm 57 years old now. If I wait another 57 years, I think that would be too long.

The point is that I have knowledge that I have wanted to share with affluent baby boomers and seniors, who are my core audience. I have wanted to share it with more people than just my clients.

The ideas in this book have been percolating in my mind for the last three years. If you do not have a close, effective, and successful relationship with your financial advisor, some of the blame may lie with you. Not to sound harsh, but it takes work on both your parts. I will show you how you might improve your relationship with your financial advisor so that it is more rewarding for you. Together, you can forge those bonds of steel.

I have gained the perspective and insights to say confidently, "Listen to what I have to share with you." If you invest your time to read these chapters and absorb these ideas, you will benefit. My hope is that my experience will resonate with you and help you to make the best possible decisions in working with your financial advisor.

MY HOPE IS THAT MY EXPERIENCE WILL RESONATE WITH YOU AND HELP YOU TO MAKE THE BEST POSSIBLE DECISIONS IN WORKING WITH YOUR FINANCIAL ADVISOR.

There are many families out there that could benefit from what I have learned in my career. I have assisted hundreds of families, and I have learned valuable lessons. As I listened to Tony Robbins at a multiday conference, I remember writing down his words in my journal: "If I don't get those ideas out, the ideas are going to die on my lips." I don't want my ideas to die on my lips.

I want this book to be a conversation starter. I hope to heighten your awareness and raise critical questions that could determine whether you have an adequate or an exceptional alliance with your advisor. I want to show you the real value of a relationship with an advisor that is deep and trusting. I have witnessed what happens in great relationships, and there is no reason it should not happen for you.

CHAPTER 2

THE VALUE OF A COACH

"I WORK AT TREATING EVERYONE WITH RESPECT. I EXPECT TO BE TREATED WITH RESPECT. I AM WILLING TO POINT THAT OUT, IF NECESSARY."

DAN S. KENNEDY

Six out of every seven days, I am at the gym—cardio three or four times a week and weight lifting three times a week. I have a coach, and although he was born and bred in the Bronx, I don't hold that against him much.

Brian Williams weighs in at 233 pounds. Most of that is solid muscle. He leads me through my weight lifting like a marine. I sweat, groan, push, pull, tremble, and complain. I guess I am making up for lost time: In the four years I was in college, I didn't even know where the gym was.

Brian pushes me to do things I would not do by myself. That is precisely why I pay him. I have made significant progress over the two years we have been working together— remarkable progress, no, but significant, yes.

I liken the work of a financial consultant to that of a coach. I watch people in my gym and other gyms perform weight exercises in a dangerous manner, swinging dumbbells in ways that will eventually end up in injury. Brian shows me how to do the exercises properly, with correct form, targeting the right muscles. He does not want to see me injured.

BRIAN SHOWS ME HOW TO DO THE EXERCISES PROPERLY, WITH CORRECT FORM, TARGETING THE RIGHT MUSCLES. HE DOES NOT WANT TO SEE ME INJURED.

If I were to hurt myself, I would have to cancel the workouts, and he wouldn't get his pay. It's a symbiotic relationship. We both win: I grow stronger, lose weight, and build muscle mass, and Brian earns his money.

This arrangement works because I am coachable. We have a constructive relationship. I benefit from his specialized knowledge and skills. I trust his experience and judgment to assist me in reaching my goals. In my business, I have seen the portfolios of many do-it-yourselfers who feel they do not need a consultant, advisor, or coach. Some of these portfolios are well constructed, others, not so much.

Common sense tells me to look at it this way. If you have a combined portfolio value (with joint accounts, IRAs, trusts, etc.) of $2 million to $4 million, that's about the size of a cash management account of a small manufacturing company. The owners of such companies hire a chief financial officer because they understand that their expertise does not extend to managing the cash assets of the firm. The owners' expertise is in manufacturing valves or widgets or little plastic buttons. In other matters, other people provide the know-how.

I hire Brian Williams because his expertise is valuable to me and I know that my outcome will be better with his help. The benefits that I receive far outweigh what I pay. I have learned that people do much better work with a coach than without one.

THE "I GET IT" MOMENT

Once, during a client-discovery session, I sat in a conference room taking copious notes. I had been brought in to provide the gray-haired perspective, helping a younger advisor who was at the session with me.

During the meeting, I looked over at this young man. He was chatting away with the clients, but he was writing nothing down. He was engaged in conversation, but he didn't appear to be listening to anyone but himself. Meanwhile, I was writing down point after point that I thought I should keep in mind if we were to do a good job. Evidently, the younger advisor next to me did not think that way at all.

When your advisor repeats back to you what you said, that indicates he or she is actively listening. You feel understood, and that's when the look passes between you, an unmistakable look of "I get it." This is an aha! moment, when a link in the chain of trust and understanding has been forged. I had that moment with those clients that day. The other advisor didn't come close. Be certain that your advisor "gets it."

ACCOUNTABILITY FLOWS BOTH WAYS

As an avid reader, I have taken in most everything that Dr. Tom Stanley has written, including his famous book *The Millionaire Next Door*, cowritten with William Danko. The book talks about people with a "big hat and skinny cattle"— people who have all the trappings of wealth, but not wealth. The book challenges our perceptions about wealth, and I recommend it without reservation.

The "big-hat-and-skinny-cattle" people might have a late-model Mercedes, Lexus, or BMW, along with a big car loan. They have a beautiful home, with a large first mortgage and an equally large home-equity line of credit. They have virtually no equity in the home. They go on expensive vacations, own Rolexes, and have all of the trappings of the wealthy, except the investment accounts, the bonds, the equities, the commercial operations, and the real estate. The balance sheet does not spell success, despite the outward signs of wealth.

Seasoned advisors will need to see that balance sheet. They need to find out just what's under that big hat. If you and your advisor are to collaborate and agree on a common purpose, you must be forthright from the outset. You must do your part in reaching the goals that you and your financial advisor have agreed upon. To create a financial plan, your advisor will need your answers to many questions about your objectives and resources. The advisor will also require from you personal documents that are essential for a comprehensive review.

IF YOU AND YOUR ADVISOR ARE TO COLLABO- RATE AND AGREE ON A COMMON PURPOSE, YOU MUST BE FORTHRIGHT FROM THE OUTSET.

I often tell clients that this is their homework. For example, if we have agreed to complete a comprehensive financial plan, there are certain specific items I will need to review and analyze:

- A copy of the most recent tax return, including W2 or 1099 information

- A copy of all bank, CD, and money market account statements

- Mutual fund, investment, IRA accounts, 401(K) accounts and corporate benefit statements

- Pension or annuity arrangements

     ℰ Long-term-care and life-insurance statements

     ℰ Disability, liability umbrella, car- and home-insurance statements

Without these documents, it is nearly impossible to create a baseline of where you are now and to chart a course to where you want to be. Your advisor will need to discover where you may be vulnerable and the reasonable steps that may be taken to mitigate the risks you face. An advisor isn't being nosy when asking for these items. Your homework is essential if the job is to be done properly.

Together, you are envisioning a comprehensive financial plan. That's a big undertaking with a significant commitment of time and expertise on the part of your advisor. You must collaborate. If you aren't forthcoming with the documents, perhaps you and the advisor aren't in sync. If your advisor or staff has to ask you repeatedly for the raw data and simple records that could be mailed, this is not a good use of their time. The advisor might wonder if you really want to get this done.

I recognize that everyone gets busy. My point is that accountability flows both ways. If you make a commitment to your advisor, you must keep it, just as you expect your advisor to keep a commitment to you. Your advisor's job is to guide and assist you in formulating a plan. It is a coaching relationship worth enhancing and preserving, but it takes two to make it happen.

There is a wide range of attitudes and philosophies in the wealth management and financial planning business. I have met hundreds of well-meaning, honest, and intelligent prac-titioners, and I've met those concerned with the next sale. My fervent hope is that the selfish people who do not embrace service to others, who have no thirst for knowledge and personal development, will be weeded out of the industry. The motivational speaker Zig Ziglar said your attitude, not your aptitude, determines your altitude. You control how high you will go, what you will achieve.

WIDE WORLD OF WEALTH MANAGEMENT

When you are having a discussion with your financial advisor, you may be reviewing many aspects of planning, which may involve your investments, insurance, retirement plans, health plans, and so on.

My industry has lumped this into a big equation called wealth management. This encompasses both the accumulation stage and the distribution stage of your life. Very simply, that means that when you are younger, you are accumulating assets for retirement. When you're older, in retirement, you are distributing those assets that you have been accumulating.

You and your advisor will also talk about the liability side of the equation. This might be lines of credit, loans, or mortgages that you may have for yourself or for other family members.

When we talk about wealth management, we are talking about a very broad category. We're talking about a myriad of other subjects that touch on your financial life. You will face a spectrum of changing concerns as you move through life.

You need the assistance of a wise advisor along the way.

A DAY IN THE LIFE

The following is fairly representative of a normal day for the advisors I have met. The most effective advisors do not have their feet up on the desk reading the *Wall Street Journal* for an hour. To be successful, a financial advisor must spend a fair amount of time thinking and reading, as well as meeting clients or talking with them on the phone. The advisor will also spend time prospecting for new clients.

- ✓ **7:30 to 9:15 a.m.** Begin work on the day's top project. Review global news headlines. Review all accounts for deposits, withdrawals, purchases, and sales. Meet with staff to review all completed, pending, and new tasks in support of clients.

- ✓ **9:30 to 11 a.m.** Make outgoing client calls. Transcribe notes on all conversations and commitments.

- ✓ **11:15 to 11:45 a.m.** Return calls.

- ✓ **12:00 to 1:15 p.m.** Attend client lunch meeting.

- ✓ **1:30 to 2:15 p.m.** Make outgoing client calls. Transcribe notes on all conversations and commitments.

- ✓ **2:30 to 4 p.m.** Attend client meeting.

- ✓ **4:15 to 5:00** p.m. Make outgoing client calls. Transcribe all notes.

- ✓ **5:15 p.m.** Go to the gym for exercise.

- ✓ **6:30 p.m.** Home with the family.

Many advisors tell me that their days are never the same or boring. In a week's time, your advisor may have been involved in the following activities:

- ✓ Arrange a bridge loan for the purchase of real estate.

- ✓ Collateralize assets to assist clients in securing cheaper financing or refinancing for properties for their children.

- ✓ Host a series of educational calls on subjects ranging from annuities, long-term-care insurance, college savings programs, municipal bond portfolios, or tax-advantaged life insurance strategies.

- ✓ Assist in updating cost basis of securities inherited due to death of a client's family member.

- ✓ Invite a client to golf or tennis.

- ✓ Assist in the transfer of assets between financial institutions.

- ✓ Assist in securing a more favorable rate on a client mortgage.

- ✓ Craft a portfolio of mutual funds or exchange traded funds.

- ✓ Discuss and review a client's 401(k) plan asset allocation (or lack of one).

- ✓ Assist in the creation of comprehensive financial and estate plans.

- ✓ Review and make recommendations on existing client insurance programs.

- ✓ Give guidance for client's daughter entering the job market.

- ✓ Engage in a conference call with client's CPAs and attorneys.

- ✓ Speak or meet with new prospects.

- ✓ Attend a client funeral.

Every successful advisor I have ever met plans his or her day ahead of time and sticks to a schedule. Considering the magnitude of the work to be done, if they were not efficient in their work habits, they would drown in a sea of to-dos.

THE SIREN SONG OF THE E-MAIL

Whether an advisor uses a day planner, a computer, or a legal pad, the important thing is to plan out the day and stick to that plan as much as possible. This can prove to be a challenge when you consider the amount of calls, e-mails, and, for some, tweets and text messages.

The time management books I have studied, written by Brian Tracy, taught me that I must master my own agenda or surrender to someone else's agenda. In other words, I must tackle the most important tasks on my to-do list first or I will never accomplish what I believe to be the most important.

For that reason, I tackle the most complex and important tasks first thing. I am aware that I might have 30 e-mails waiting for me, but if I made a commitment to a client that I would complete a project by a certain date, that must take priority. It might surprise you to know that it is not uncommon for an advisor to receive 60 to 80 e-mails a day. Each of those comes from someone trying to ask a question, inform, or sell something.

No matter the weather, time of year, or sickness, the e-mails just keep on coming. They have become what Dan Kennedy calls "time vampires."

Sometimes, I must ignore, for the time being, the beeping from the inbox and have my calls sent to my assistant or a voicemail system. I cannot compromise my productivity because of a stream of e-mails that never stops. For this reason, *it is important for you to understand* and appreciate that your advisor may not e-mail you a reply or respond to your message immediately. It likely will come in a reasonable period of time, but do not wait by your machine in anticipation. Sometimes, I think that people imagine I am gazing into my computer, waiting for them to e-mail me, and then I can reply within seconds. Efficient use of time? Not by a long shot.

SOMETIMES, I MUST IGNORE, FOR THE TIME BEING, THE BEEPING FROM THE INBOX.

I have tried to structure my day so I can focus on e-mails twice: once in the morning and once in the afternoon. I am the first to admit that it is hard to do. The siren song of the e-mail is hard to resist, but the more I do so, the more my productivity rises.

If a meteor is streaking toward the Washington metropolitan area, I most likely will not receive the news by e-mail. Most probably, I will see some of my colleagues running and screaming down the hallway. Do not get upset if your advisor does not instantly respond to your message. My sense is that you will hear back as your advisor's schedule allows. After all, you wouldn't want to be a nudge, would you?

STAYING IN CONTACT

I firmly believe that it is in a client's best interest to share emergency contact information, perhaps the name and phone number or e-mail address of a son, daughter, brother, or sister. The reason is simple: from time to time, it comes to the attention of an advisor that someone might be taking advantage of an elderly client.

This happens mostly when the elderly client lives alone. Telltale signs include an increase in requests for cash from an account or requests that are out of character for the client. This may include third-party check requests or the wiring of funds to an unfamiliar account. Your advisor would love to be able to pick up the phone to ask your family member to check on you. Do not take this advice for granted. The problem is real, and it occurs often with seniors.

Whether you are a senior or a baby boomer on your way to the ranks of senior, if you have a relatively new relationship with your financial advisor, you might have a conversation focusing on what you did not like about your prior financial advisory relationship. By diplomatically explaining what it was about your prior advisor you did not like, you are in effect giving your current advisor a road map for how to have a successful relationship with you. For example, you may wish to receive a call each month from your advisor with updates on specific items.

If the conversation with your current advisor highlights the fact that the prior advisor called only every 90 days, and you felt that was not enough, you can conclude that you'd feel much better if you were updated every month. I have found that misunderstandings happen because there were not enough directions, questions, and listening.

If you wish your advisor to do something, *you must tell him or her.* Please do not assume your advisor will know what you're thinking.

PARALYZING FEAR

From time to time, all advisors have had to deal with circumstances where, based on their training and experience, they are aware that certain actions should be taken. However, that does not mean that the person who should take those actions is willing to do so.

Your advisor would explain that the intention is to protect you and bring about more certainty in your financial life. However, intention alone cannot fix things. There must be a willingness.

Donald and Frances (not their real names), acquaintances of a mutual friend, were not clients of my practice. Donald was all about immediate gratification. Frances was all about careful planning and preparation. Donald, a high-end computer services professional, routinely received large bonuses for the exemplary work he did for Fortune 500 companies. Each time he received a bonus, he wanted to take an extravagant vacation or buy fancy toys. Frances, however, wanted to stash the funds away to build their nest egg and save for their retirement.

As they decided early on in their marriage not to have kids, no funds were needed for college education. Over time, Frances assumed responsibility for paying all of the bills and overseeing their investments. Donald toyed with his computers and spent his time off writing spy novels that never sold. Frances became adept at planning nice vacations that were inexpensive and tucking away thousands and thousands of dollars into their investment and retirement accounts.

Donald was clueless about this. When asked about planning for retirement, he always replied that there was plenty of time for that. Evidently, when it came to talking about money, they simply didn't. Frances was in charge of their financial lives, and Donald was fine with that. Eventually, Frances and Donald accumulated a significant investment and retirement portfolio of approximately $2.2 million.

One day, it occurred to Frances that she did not have the knowledge and experience to properly manage a nest egg of that size. Although she felt that she picked blue chip stocks that had good write-ups in popular financial magazines, the financial meltdown in 2008 and 2009 produced portfolio losses of nearly $800,000. She panicked and placed everything in cash after she concluded that much of the magazine recommendations were just doubletalk.

Donald was blissfully unaware that anything was wrong. He would come home, they would share dinner, and he would retire to his study to work on his novels. By now, Frances was distressed and anxious about their money. She had no experience with such emotions.

She decided to get professional help. She met with an experienced advisor alone, telling the advisor that Donald had no interest in such meetings. The advisor accepted her as a client and, after several meetings, laid out a plan of action for her and Donald. The intention of the advisor was to get Frances and Donald to a position where they would have guaranteed sources of income in retirement, with a potential for growth in the six years before Donald retired.

Everything that the advisor laid out was reasonable and appropriate for their situation. Frances took the recommendations, reviewed them carefully, and did nothing. After a while, she no longer returned the advisor's calls asking her to take action. The advisor was under the impression that Frances had a willingness to move forward and to implement his recommendations. But deep inside, Frances could not forgive herself for losing that $800,000. She put all of their funds in CDs that were paying less than 1 percent interest.

Frances and her advisor never got on the same page. The advisor never understood that she was frozen with fear over their financial situation and did not have a willingness to take any action at all. I have seen similar scenarios unfold. Slammed by hard times, people sometimes retreat to cash and money markets permanently. ○

HOW TO BE A GOOD PARTNER

When you have a relationship with a financial advisor, it is incumbent upon you to be a good partner. By that, I mean you want to participate in the decision-making process.

Many times during my career, I have heard these words, "Just do what you think best." Don't get me wrong. It was said with honest intentions and a great deal of trust. However, one of the more important tenets of the wealth management industry is that an advisor must not take discretion unless it is granted by the client in advance in writing and approved by the firm that employs the advisor. There are a host of regulations that govern this.

By discretion, I mean that the advisor may not make purchases or sales in clients' accounts that are not discussed and approved ahead of time. Advisors understand that clients may not want to be involved in the nitty-gritty details of portfolio management. However, advisors do have an obligation to do their very best to involve the clients and inform them of all pertinent details and risks. Above all, the strategy considered must be suitable and appropriate for the client.

When a client says, "Just do what you think is best," that tells me that the client does not wish to be involved in efforts involving his or her own finances. It comes across, in a sense, as meaning the client does not want to think. You do not want to place your advisor in that position.

"JUST DO WHAT YOU THINK IS BEST," COMES ACROSS, IN A SENSE, AS MEANING THE CLIENT DOES NOT WANT TO THINK.

Advisors seek to inform, to educate, to guide, and to assist, but you are the boss. We may act in the role of chief investment officer, but you are the chief executive officer. We are here to help you. We cannot make the decisions for you. They are yours to make. It's when I'm involved in a collaborative effort, with questions and answers and discussions back and forth, that I absolutely love my work.

ADVISORS SEEK TO INFORM, TO EDUCATE, TO GUIDE, AND TO ASSIST, BUT YOU ARE THE BOSS.

Basically, you have to be coachable. If you think, for example, that you have superior knowledge because you watched a television program or read an article, you are on shaky ground. You need to be able to accept professional guidance. People who do what I do have availed themselves of thousands of hours of learning and experience. They have acquired the expertise to serve you and your family.

A good advisor or advisory team will listen carefully to you before offering suggestions for your financial well-being and will see you through from beginning to end. Unlike the talking heads on television, your advisor should have a personal understanding of your unique situation, needs, and goals. *A good advisor is aware of your family dynamics. It's a sorely needed perspective that derives from a true relationship and one that you cannot get from the mass media.* The financial magazines can publish their top-ten lists, but none of them necessarily reflects your personal priorities and what is best for you.

THANKS BUT NO THANKS

Perhaps you have a passion for something that would bore the heck out of others. Maybe it's growing tomatoes in your backyard, arranging family photos in beautiful keepsake albums, or collecting unusual postage stamps. I would wager that your advisor might have some pet investment passions as well.

This comes close to home. Let's say that as part of your comprehensive investment strategy, a portion of your assets are to be allocated to tax-free municipal bonds. I know many advisors who are quite knowledgeable about bonds and could speak for hours on the subject. They can differentiate between general obligation and revenue bonds or delve into the difference between a bond mutual fund and owning an individual bond.

Often such advisors are only too happy to pass on all that knowledge to you. But I learned a long time ago that people do not care how much an advisor knows until they know how much that advisor cares. It might be enough that your advisor gives you the light version of the benefits of municipal bonds without trying to make you an expert. Clients have told me that they are comfortable that I possess the knowledge. It is not their desire to possess it as well.

It's like the talented athlete who trusts that his coach has what it takes to bring out the best in him.

CHAPTER 3

FINANCIAL ADVISOR ESSENTIALS

"THE ONLY WAY YOU CAN FIND
OUT WHETHER YOU CAN TRUST
SOMEBODY IS TO TRUST HIM."

BRIAN GARFIELD

"In the meantime, and in between time," my stepmom, Shirley Friedman, would say as she watched the employees at Norton's Laundry. And often she directed those words at me as she held me accountable for using my time wisely.

I remember observing her while she worked with my dad in running the laundry. She would survey the factory floor with a keen eye. Shirley could perform every job in the place. She knew every machine, every task, and every function. Norton's had dozens of employees, and she knew how long it took to do each task. She knew if employees deliberately took their time in completing the tasks assigned to them.

Shirley taught me the importance of clarity of thought, a concept that Brian Tracy, years later, also would teach me. Many times, she would look me right in the eye and intone, "Forget all that crap. What are you trying to say?" For these lessons, I'm very grateful. Shirley taught me how to cut through the unimportant and get to the important—and get it done. As my dad did, she emphasized that if you have something to do, just do it. I suspect that each of them were tired of seeing some of their employees moving aimlessly through life, never improving their situation. I am grateful that they didn't want me to end up that way.

SHIRLEY TAUGHT ME HOW TO CUT THROUGH THE UNIMPORTANT AND GET TO THE IMPORTANT—AND GET IT DONE. AS MY DAD DID, SHE EMPHASIZED THAT IF YOU HAVE SOMETHING TO DO, JUST DO IT.

Shirley had perspective, gained from years of experience working with my father. Her experience was indispensable in helping to guide the best decisions on the future course of the business. Shirley is smart as a whip and still able to size up situations and act accordingly by using her insights. I'm blessed to still have her here in my life and the lives of my entire family.

Shirley is what many people call street smart. I know today that she played a major role in drilling into me some of the essential values that make up a good financial advisor.

COMPETENCE

When advisors are unsure of themselves, it comes through. By that, I mean a seasoned advisor has dealt with many clients with numerous problems. He or she may have dealt with such problems dozens of times, coming to know just what needs to happen to solve an issue and when.

When presented with a set of facts, new advisors may not recognize what they are dealing with, or its importance. That's why I feel that an experienced financial advisor is the best answer for someone in need of retirement income and financial planning.

As I emphasized earlier, financial advisors should be very well read. They must have a self-imposed minimum reading requirement. I've run into many financial advisors, over the years, who have had plenty of time for friends but could not tell you about the last book they had read on economics or retirement planning.

One of the best ways to forge close bonds between you and your advisor is through the use of deep questions. There are hundreds, perhaps thousands, of questions an advisor might ask you, and hopefully, they will be open-ended questions that do not allow for a simple yes or no answer.

**ONE OF THE BEST WAYS TO FORGE CLOSE
BONDS BETWEEN YOU AND YOUR ADVISOR IS
THROUGH THE USE OF DEEP QUESTIONS.**

Such questions are important to developing an understanding of who you are and what is important to you. Hopefully, when you began your current relationship, you were not blindsided by something like this: "Hi, I thought it would be helpful to get your answers to these 235 questions. It shouldn't take long. Let's get started, okay?"

Now take a look at the following brief list of questions. It is not exhaustive by any means. They are designed to foster conversation and lead your advisor to understand more about you.

- *Tell me about your family.*

- *Financially speaking, what do you want to do for your kids or grandkids?*

- *What did you learn about money when you were growing up, and who did you learn it from?*

- *What were the best and worst financial investments you ever made? Why?*

- *What do you like to spend money on?*

- *Tell me about the type of investments that you have experience with.*

- *Tell me about the insurance coverage you've put in place for you and your family.*

℘ *What type of estate-planning documents do you have in place, and how old are they?*

℘ *What steps have you taken, if any, to safeguard your retirement nest egg from the risks of catastrophic health-care costs?*

℘ *Have you ever engaged in a beneficiary review of all your insurance, annuity, retirement, and benefit programs?*

℘ *Tell me about the dreams and goals you have for your spouse, your kids, your grandkids.*

℘ *Have there been any previous marriages for you or your spouse, and are there children from a previous marriage?*

℘ *Are there any specific concerns that you have about any family members?*

℘ *Many advisory relationships begin or become stronger due to a recent triggering event. Has anything significant occurred in your family or business situation recently?*

℘ *Think about this for a moment, have you felt it necessary to assist your adult children financially? What were the circumstances and results?*

℘ *Ideally, what amount of income would you think is reasonable for your portfolio to produce annually?*

℘ *How often have you had to make unanticipated withdrawals from your investment account, and how recent was this?*

℘ *I want to know, in your own words, what you think is your tolerance for risk.*

℘ *How can we add more value to our relationship?*

EMPATHY

The advisor must have enough life and career experience to understand what people go through. What do they aspire to accomplish? What are their dreams and their worries and struggles? I have met very few 22-year-olds who can add value in this realm.

Financial advisors must have their antennae up. They must be willing and able to connect with what their clients and prospects are telling them, and they need to be ready for their tears and their anger as people discuss the regrets and frustrations of their lives. This is an emotional business.

The advisor has to develop an approach that helps clients to feel comfortable in discussing difficult matters. The client needs to understand that the advisor truly cares and is not there for a transaction. I have seen strong emotions welling up in people, and I know that those are times when it is more important than ever that I focus on, and come to understand, the source of those feelings. With empathy and understanding we can find the best path together.

THE ADVISOR HAS TO DEVELOP AN APPROACH THAT HELPS CLIENTS TO FEEL COMFORTABLE IN DIS-CUSSING DIFFICULT MATTERS. THE CLIENT NEEDS TO UNDERSTAND THAT THE ADVISOR TRULY CARES AND IS NOT THERE FOR A TRANSACTION.

ABILITY TO LISTEN

"You have two ears and one mouth," my mother, Lyla Ruth Friedman, often told me. She made it clear to me that I should be listening twice as much as I was talking, and her advice has served me well in my life and career.

"YOU HAVE TWO EARS AND ONE MOUTH," MY MOTHER, LYLA RUTH FRIEDMAN, OFTEN TOLD ME.

If an advisor does most of the talking when meeting with a client, or if the advisor talks over the client, there's a problem. Clients come to an advisor for professional expertise, but they don't want to be lectured.

The conversation should flow easily both ways as advisor and client get to the heart of matters in an atmosphere of mutual respect. If the advisor is monopolizing the conversation by speaking 90 percent of the time, something is wrong.

Dan Sullivan is one of the foremost business coaches on the planet. I have read much of his material, and he asks a question that has been burned into my mind, "If we were having this conversation three years from today, and you were looking back over those three years, what has to have happened in your life both personally and professionally for you to feel happy with your progress?"

In my continuing discovery process with clients, I have found it helpful to dig, to question, and to clarify, working to understand critical issues in the mind of my clients. This is accomplished by the art of listening, and some of the smartest people in my industry have emphasized its importance.

The best consultants—and I hope that includes yours—ask probing and open-ended questions and listen for answers. They want explanations that aid in their understanding, not simply yes and no answers. They search for clues and meaning in what you say, taking notes and exploring further. They then synthesize those ideas to get to the core of what affects you and your family.

THE ART OF GENTLE QUESTIONING

When you are engaged in a meaningful conversation with your advisor, you expect his or her full attention on what you are saying. You expect that the advisor will question you to ensure complete understanding.

Good advisors are genuine in how they communicate with you. Picture your conversation as if the two of you were tossing a little golf ball back and forth gently. Each interaction adds to understanding.

Take a look at the following hypothetical interaction between a client we will call Saul and his advisor, Benjamin:

Saul: I'm worried about leaving too much money to the kids. Who knows how they'll spend it and what will happen? I've heard and read that kids tend to make poor decisions with money they didn't earn. I think it's called the sudden wealth syndrome.

Benjamin: How do you mean, Saul? What do you see going wrong if you and Rhoda were to leave money to the kids? Please tell me more.

Saul: Well, Ben, I guess my imagination kicks into overdrive. I can see Gina, my youngest, buying a fancy red sports car. Carl—he's the one who dropped out of college—I can see him taking a six-month vacation in the Caribbean to find himself. And as for Dennis, my oldest, I could see a divorce in his future, with my daughter-in-law walking away with half of what I leave him.

The best consultants as probing and open-ended questions and listen for answers to get to the core of what affects you and your family.

I just think that leaving them money to do with as they please might do more harm than good. I want my kids to benefit from our success, but I'm scared of making mistakes.

Benjamin: Saul, if I hear you right, you love your kids and you want what's best for them, but somehow you want to place constraints and suggest some guidelines as to how their inheritance money is to be used. You're worried they will make what you consider to be bad choices.

Saul: Exactly, Ben. You got it. Tell me, am I the only one with this kind of issue?

Benjamin: Saul, I've worked with a number of families over the years, and by no means are you alone in this. Tell me, if you were able to leave money to Gina, Carl, and Dennis but somehow erect fences around it so they made smart choices, would you want to talk more about that?

Saul: You bet. That's exactly what I want to achieve, but I haven't the faintest idea how to do that.

Benjamin: My team and I are happy to help, and we have some ideas that you may find useful. First, I'd like you to chat with Rhoda to get a general idea of what the two of you consider good uses and poor uses of money. Grab a sheet of paper and make a list. For example, enrolling in graduate school versus buying a boat, or buying investment real estate versus buying a Porsche, or buying a home versus taking an expensive European vacation. Once you have done that, the three of us will get together again and see what you agree on and the outcomes that are comfortable for the both of you.

At that point, I'll give you further guidance on what you'll want to do next. If we need specialized assistance for some issues, I have a network of experienced colleagues we can bring in for help.

Saul: Ben, thank you. You really listen and understand what we're worried about, what keeps us up at night. Rhoda and I are grateful for your guidance. You know, some of our friends spend their days on their computer buying and selling every time CNBC says boo. With you, we get a comprehensive financial plan, a well-thought-out strategy. It means a lot to us, Ben.

Ben: I appreciate your kind words, Saul.

You may look at this as Benjamin joining the conversation that's already going on in Saul and Rhoda's head. By listening and discussing how they feel about an inheritance that they may leave to their kids and understanding what their fears are, *Benjamin can now render meaningful advice.*

Do you think that he will recommend that they speak in the near future with an experienced estate-planning attorney? I would think so.

TWO-WAY COMMUNICATION

A good relationship with an advisor requires active engagement. Your partnership is a two-way street. Communication has to flow each way. Granted, you will need to listen, but you also want to ask questions that will engage your advisor's intellect. When I am actively listening to people and trying to absorb everything they say, I lean in, look them in the eye, and focus. I try to tune everything else out. I won't be fiddling with my cell phone or jingling change in my pocket.

So many times over the years, I have found myself hoping that clients would ask certain questions of me. Those questions tell me they are paying attention and are actively engaged in the conversation. When I find these questions are not forthcoming, I will say something like the following:

"A number of families whom I work with and who have implemented the same strategy we're discussing today asked if there were any surrender or termination charges on this program. I thought this would be something that you would want to be aware of as well. Am I correct?"

Sometimes people have to be guided to ask the right questions. The client should feel free to ask the advisor, "What are the questions that people like me ask?" or "What are the things I should be asking you that I don't know to ask?" I guess many consultants and advisors might be happy that the questions did not come up. As for me, I like to cover all bases, so if a client does not bring up important points for discussion, I will.

My point is you want to make sure that your advisor takes the time to explain to you what needs to be explained. You want to be confident that your advisor and his team have experience in dealing with people like you. After all, you are trusting them with the oversight and monitoring of your assets.

I have known planners and consultants who specialize in dealing with dentists, or with architects, or with authors. These professionals like to focus on one or two niches, and they become highly knowledgeable about the challenges facing those groups.

That way, they can offer their clients reassurance of expertise with issues specific to those professionals. The advisor can say, "I have dealt with dozens of people who do what you do, and I have assisted these people with solutions to many of the problems you probably face in your business."

TRAVELING THE SAME PATH

Over the years, I have seen many of my clients on the same journey that I am on, traveling the same path. Some have been further down the road, facing new challenges along the way as their children prepare to leave the nest. My own children are at that stage. Jason soon will begin his college years. He hopes to play basketball for a Division 1 school. As I write this, he has just accomplished 1,000 career points in high school and is the top three-point shooter in the region. Avery is finishing four years of undergraduate work in psychology and hopes to pursue a master's degree in gerontology. Reena and I are extraordinarily proud of both of our children.

Some of my clients have grandchildren and want to make financial or educational arrangements for them, and we discuss what might be done. Wherever you are on your journey, make sure that your advisor understands what is important to you. After all, it's all about family, isn't it? That understanding comes by way of discussion, questioning, and listening, perhaps over a meal or a cup of coffee. Help your advisor to fully appreciate what and who is important to you and why. Remember, not all conversations are about investments. Any investments you might have are there to serve a purpose. That purpose most likely involves you and your family. Do not be afraid to discuss you and your family with your advisor.

PERSPECTIVE AND INSIGHT

The finest financial advisors I have met share an uncommon trait: perspective.

I think of perspective and insight as twins. Whenever I have seen one, the other is following right behind. I believe planners gain perspective and insight through thousands of hours of listening, collaborating, advising, and acting as a steward of the financial assets and dreams of the families they serve.

I've often heard it said that people with perspective and insight see with their intellect. They possess vision. In my career, I have met a handful of extraordinary people with those traits. They are beyond smart. When you find yourself in a room with them, you feel like picking up your pencil and taking notes.

One of them is Steve Gresham, an author, speaker, and executive in the wealth management industry. I have heard Steve speak numerous times to audiences of financial advisors and management. I have read all of his books—twice—and count him as a friend.

In his book *The New Advisor for Life: Become the Indispensable Financial Advisor to Affluent Families*, he wrote: "Perspective based on the experience of others is among the most important criteria cited by clients for why they selected their financial advisor. 'Have you ever worked with anyone like me?' is a dominant query."

During my time as a financial consultant with Smith Barney, I was fortunate to have Michael Maurer as a supervisor, branch manager, and complex director. In lengthy discussions with Mike, I realized his phenomenal ability to synthesize and verbalize the concepts I was trying to verbalize. He is excellent at reading people and excels in situational awareness.

Time and again, he'd ask me about issues that I should have brought up but hadn't. For example, we would talk about marketing strategy, and he would cue me in on steps I had not even considered. His influence made the plan better than I had envisioned.

As an experienced advisor and manager, Mike's perspective and insight were highly developed. One of his responsibilities was to build a branch office of honest, ethical, caring, and trustworthy advisors. Not only did he succeed but he also did a marvelous job.

CHAPTER 4

A FOUNDATION OF TRUST

"TRUST, BUT VERIFY."

RUSSIAN PROVERB, OFTEN CITED BY
PRESIDENT RONALD REAGAN

A number of times throughout my career, I have come face to face with professional investment incompetence. Each time I see it, I experience two emotions.

The first is anger. I am offended that a professional within my industry would create a poorly designed portfolio that violates even the most basic rules of asset allocation and common sense. The second emotion I feel is compassion for the victim of that incompetence, who has had to live with the consequences.

When I sit down and review the investment statements, I am outwardly calm and professional, taking notes and asking questions. But inside, I feel like yelling at the person responsible. For example, the entire portfolio might be real estate investment trusts, or it might consist entirely of preferred stocks or annuities. I wonder what that advisor was thinking. Where's the proper diversification? Surely, the advisor could have done a better job, but it seems as if that didn't matter.

All investment professionals across the land have a duty to do the right thing. Even without consulting the Securities and Exchange Commission rules, they know the difference between right and wrong. I came up with my own guideline when dealing with older retirees, which I call the mother rule, and it's simple: if it would not be placed in my mom's portfolio, it will not be placed in yours.

·I CAME UP WITH MY OWN GUIDELINE, WHICH I CALL THE MOTHER RULE, AND IT'S SIMPLE: IF IT WOULD NOT BE PLACED IN MY MOM'S PORTFOLIO, IT WILL NOT BE PLACED IN YOURS.

I think of this as akin to the creed of the medical professional whose oath commands, "First, do no harm." Those are important words for all investment professionals to remember. I'm not saying this from any bully pulpit. Advisors can do very serious long-term financial harm if they do not practice their craft with intelligence, integrity, and skill.

In time, I feel two additional emotions: a sense of relief and a sense of closure. Those feelings come after I have fixed the issues that I see in the portfolio, reallocating assets in a suitable and appropriate manner that supports the client's objectives and tolerance for risk. I have made a poor situation better and made a real difference in the client's life. I can smile and look the client in the eye and say that together we have completed all of the changes that needed to happen. Now, we can focus on monitoring the portfolio.

WHERE TRUST BEGINS

The acquisition of knowledge does not ensure that your advisor will be trustworthy. Trustworthiness is a very different attribute. You have to figure out if the person you are dealing with is worthy of your trust.

During my career, I have heard stories of clients who have trusted an advisor with only a small portion of their assets—perhaps $50,000, but not $500,000. I suppose that's meant as a test for how the advisor will handle the funds, but I find this kind of thinking flawed. When I think of diversification, I think of a variety of asset classes or individual securities. I don't think of advisor diversification.

My sense is that playing one advisor against another and seeing how each of them does may be a fool's errand. In a poor market environment, would the winning advisor be the one who lost only 16 percent of your capital versus the advisor who lost 21 percent? Or perhaps in a strong market, would the best advisor be the one who generated less taxable capital gains?

At some point, we must bow to the absurd. If your trusted family financial advisor is designing a strategy just for you, what would be the point of having two—or, for heaven's sake, three—individually crafted and personalized financial plans?

A FEELING OF KINSHIP

I like to characterize forging bonds of trust with open communications and frank and honest discussions between you and your advisor, with an easy give and take. These interactions should not be strained or forced.

I don't pretend to be some guardian of the secrets to trusted relationships or that I can teach you all the dos and the don'ts. I just consistently try to do the best I can, as we all do.

My father would say that this is where common sense takes over. There is no set of laws to follow, no absolutes. When I think of laws, I think of gravity. You may not be aware of the law of gravity, you may not even like the law of gravity, but I guarantee you that if you step off the roof of a building you will become intimately familiar with gravity. This is an absolute.

Now think of how you and a good friend of yours established trust. It didn't come with immediate, unwavering certainty. It was done over time, little by little. The trust built on itself like a snowball tumbling down a hill and adding mass as it covered the distance.

I guarantee you that if you step off the roof of a building you will become intimately familiar with gravity. This is an absolute.

Perhaps you share things in common. The list of possibilities could be endless. In my experience, my clients and I began to forge bonds in easy ways, such as these:

- You went to State College? So did I.

- You grew up in New York City? I love New York City.

- Your son plays basketball? So does mine.

- Your wife is from Missouri? I'm from there. Where did she live?

- You vacationed in St. Maarten? So did I. Where did you stay?

🔗 Your grandparents came from Russia? So did mine.

🔗 Your daughter goes to college in Virginia? So does mine. Where does she go?

I recently attended a shareholders' meeting in Manhattan. As I listened to a chief executive discuss his upbringing, I instantly felt a bond with him. He was a dapper, tall gentleman in his early seventies. He stood there in a conservative gray suit, white shirt, and red tie. He wore gold cufflinks that peeked out below the sleeve of his impeccably pressed jacket.

Why did I feel a bond with him? He grew up in New Jersey, and I grew up in New York. Not the same but very close. We were practically neighbors! He is Jewish, as am I. His grandparents came from Russia, and so did mine. His childhood hero is Superman, and I . . . Do I really need to go on?

I instantly felt a kinship with him. Granted, he is a bit older and has $1 billion more than I do, but hey, there's a commonality.

People tend to like people who are like them or how they want to be. I really would not mind being dashing and trim in my early seventies, years from now, with a billion dollars of net worth. That is definitely how I would like to be.

Do you have a commonality with your financial advisor, perhaps more than one? Think about the interesting traits that the two of you might share. It probably wouldn't be hard to name a half a dozen right now. Those are points by which you might bond for a lifetime.

A RELATIONSHIP ENDURING YEARS

The best relationships between clients and advisors are forged over years, just as your best friend was not your best friend the first, second, or third time you met. It took time to establish the rapport and trust that make up the foundation of a successful relationship.

Many times, you might say something such as, "I wish I had known that 20 years ago." For example, when saving for a child's or grandchild's education, generally speaking, the sooner you start putting money away, the less money you will have to put into the investment.

These are some things that may be common knowledge for an investment advisor, but they're not part of laypeople's world. It's not part of their thinking.

What's important is that the advisor, over the years, behaves in an ethical and responsible manner so that the client's interests come first, second, and third. You must feel confident that the advisor is there to help your family achieve what is important to you.

THE CLIENT'S INTERESTS COME FIRST, SECOND, AND THIRD.

The magic ingredients are time and effort, on both your part and your advisor's. That's why it's very important for you and your advisor to spend some time together, not only on the phone but at meetings and other get-togethers. I have been involved for decades with some families, from parent to child to grandchild.

You may discuss legacy issues, gifting, or intergenerational issues. The point is that when you're working with your financial advisor, it's about more than the rate of return, how much cash flow your portfolio throws off, or which municipal bonds you should own. Many, many meetings and discussions are spent talking about family, because family is what's important to most of us.

MANY, MANY MEETINGS AND DISCUSSIONS ARE
SPENT TALKING ABOUT FAMILY, BECAUSE FAMILY
IS WHAT'S IMPORTANT TO MOST OF US.

YOU CAN'T HANG TRUST ON A WALL

I often see an array of plaques hanging on office walls—awards for products sold or certificates for courses completed, or for this or for that. I saw one office that must have had over thirty plaques on the wall. My eyes got tired trying to take them all in.

I used to have a number of plaques hanging in my office, but I took them all down and stored them in my garage.

I have long since come to understand that it's not about me. It's not about accolades. It's about the clients and the families that I serve, and I don't need to display all of these distinctions.

Instead, I need to gain their trust and their confidence that I have the experience to do right by them. What I do have on my office wall is a collection of 21 of my business cards, beginning with my first job with E.F. Hutton and going all the way to today. Those cards are a testament to the experience that I am proud to offer my clients.

No matter what an advisor has hanging on the wall, what matters most is that he or she is trustworthy, focused, results oriented, organized, dependable, thoughtful, observant, skillful, methodical, reliable, and attentive. When you sense those qualities, you gain reassurance of a job well done. No advisor, no matter how skilled, will know all of the answers, but you should be working with a reliable guide to finding those answers.

There are few things that happen in the field of family finances that a highly experienced advisor has not run across. When a situation calls for another professional's expertise, an experienced advisor knows whom to ask. In my years as an advisor, I've heard the questions that investors ask or should be asking. Unfortunately, investors aren't aware of what they don't know—and when it comes to money, what you don't know can hurt you.

"LIFE IS FULL OF RISKS"

David Darst, in his book *The Little Book That Still Saves Your Assets: What the Rich Do to Stay Wealthy in Up and Down Markets,* said this about asset allocation, "We want to be able to mix and match assets that do not act like each other. Real estate, whether real property or real estate investment trusts, behaves differently from assets such as fixed income. Gold tends to differ in behavior from stocks. It is critical to mix and match your assets in order to smooth your overall portfolio returns."

I have heard David Darst speak a number of times, and each time, I am furiously taking notes. I have read each of his books on asset allocation including his classic text, *The Art of Asset Allocation.* Jim Cramer of CNBC fame calls him a financial visionary and knowledgeable beyond belief. I have studied Darst's writings year after year so that I can use that knowledge to construct better and more intelligent portfolios for the families I serve.

In *The Little Book That Still Saves Your Assets,* Darst says, "Asset allocation can't make risk go away. Face it. Life is full of risks, and success is not a straight line up. What asset allocation does is force you to answer some challenging questions which should lead you to a portfolio construction that will hopefully prevent you from doing something silly when things get tough or when things are going exceedingly well."

You need to be able to trust that your advisor has your back when you face those risks that surely will arise in any investor's life, whether from the economy or from your own missteps. You want an advisor who is dedicated to your success.

WHO'S MINDING THE STORE?

When I was a kid in the 1960s, my dad's bank would call him about one issue or another. It was never for a bounced check because I don't believe that my dad ever bounced a check in his life.

I believe they were service-related calls. "Can we do something for you, Mr. Friedman?" or "This kind of account will earn more interest than the one you're currently using," or "You could lower your bank fees by . . ."

When were these wonderful bank service professionals replaced with computers that no longer give wonderful service? Today, if you have an account at one of the big banks, I think you would be old before you received a personal call from a staff member. It feels as if you are no more than an account number stored in some data center in Lansing, Michigan, or in Fargo, North Dakota.

Some time ago, I was asked to assume responsibility and oversight of an elderly couple's brokerage account when their advisor left the business. The couple had their accounts at my firm for a number of years. Upon reviewing the accounts, I saw that they were invested in high-quality municipal bonds and in a money market fund.

After familiarizing myself with their accounts, I called to introduce myself and make them aware that their advisor, whom they'd used for years, had decided to leave the business. We set up an appointment to go over their various alternatives.

David and Mickey were a delightful couple who lived at a nearby golf and retirement community. They had three kids who lived around the country. Jeffrey, Gail, and Ellyn were the joys of their life.

David had worked in the federal government for decades, holding important posts in several agencies. He had a generous defined benefit plan under the old federal retirement system. Mickey was a schoolteacher for 38 years and also had a wonderful pension arrangement. In fact, their income was far more than they could spend.

Over the course of eight months, we met a number of times. I discovered the following. They had dozens of unopened envelopes on their desk. Many contained monthly statements.

They had large, six-figure balances at several banks earning 0 percent interest. They had no current wills, nor had they any legacy plan in place. The children were not involved in any aspect of their parents' financial lives.

There is an important point here that is not to be missed. Many older parents feel they do not want their grown children involved in their financial lives. I understand and respect this. Perhaps the parents feel it is none of their kids' business. Or they do not wish them to know how much they have accumulated. Sometimes they feel that one child can be of help but not another.

The withholding of important information, however, might do more harm than good. Ask yourself this: Would you think it constructive if the kids were thrust into the position overnight, upon your passing, without prepara-tion, of having to coordinate your financial matters?

Perhaps you may wish to disclose a portion of your plans to your kids, and make sure they know whom to contact in any emergency. They should know where you keep your important documents and the names of your advisor, attorney, and CPA. Maybe they should know facts you are not currently sharing with them. Talk with your advisor about what you feel comfortable doing, and by all means, let your advisor, attorney, or CPA assist you. You do not have to do all of the heavy lifting.

Back to my story: I saw in my mind all of the pieces that needed to come together to craft a strategy that would improve David and Mickey's situation. I worked with them to draw up a plan of action. I asked permission to enlist the assistance of their children. I knew that without a catalyst, nothing would change. And things certainly had to change. I assumed the role of facilitator.

You will want your financial advisor to show you how to properly allocate your assets in a way that is suitable to your station in life, and that is appropriate for your circumstances. ○

A GRAY-HAIRED PERSPECTIVE

Sometimes you just want to scream out for the experienced person in a room. There are plenty of bright young people, of course, but it gave me pause to hear the question that a young colleague asked upon hearing that one of the world's finest voices would be the surprise entertainment at a recent gathering that I attended. "So who's Barbra Streisand?" he asked.

A rabbi told me a story, once, about an elderly relative who was ill and hospitalized. This particular facility was a teaching hospital. Each time the man was examined, eight people would march into the room, each taking a turn at listening to his heartbeat and thumping his chest. Toward the middle of the group was a tall, thin fellow in his late 60s. He was clearly the head doctor with brains and experience. This was the guy in charge.

After several days of watching this entourage follow the boss around, the patient was getting quite irritated and wanted some time alone with the doctor. During one of the exams, he asked everyone under 50 years old to "get the hell out of the room."

The doctor nodded to the shocked medical students, and they all dutifully marched out. The old man in bed felt much better than he had in days. He did not like crowds. It reminded him of his Navy days aboard his ship where the sailors were crammed into bunks.

He fixed his gaze on the gray-haired doctor's eyes. In a low voice, he said, "So, without all your little medical school children running around like so many cackling chickens, I wanted to hear it from the only guy in the room with gray hair. Tell me doctor, am I going to live?"

The doctor smiled. He had heard the gray-haired reference many times before. Gray hair had become synonymous with experience. (A fact that has not been lost on the author.)

"Yes, Mr. Goldman, you will most likely live for quite a few years yet, as long as you eat right, get plenty of exercise, and look both ways before crossing the street. I'm sorry that the methods of this teaching hospital put your nerves on edge, but you know that you and I will not be around forever, and someone has to teach the next generation of doctors. Who is going to care for your children and grandchildren if we don't see to it that they get first-rate education with plenty of hands-on experience from old goats like me?"

CHEMISTRY ISN'T JUST FOR THE LAB

I have never seen a strained relationship last, whether between an advisor and client or between spouses or business partners. I liken it to being on the same page. Determining if there is a fit between you and your advisor is much more important than a superficial, "Oh, yes. We get along." The chemistry must be right.

I remember times when I did not have a good fit with clients, and eventually, they or I ended the relationship. Continuing in an advisory relationship with a poor fit is like continuing to date someone in whom you have no interest. Why perpetuate the pain? Your advisor must be there to answer your questions and to help you solve problems. You need to work with people you can rely on, and you should be comfortable with them. That kind of chemistry is out there.

CONTINUING IN AN ADVISORY RELATIONSHIP WITH A POOR FIT IS LIKE CONTINUING TO DATE SOMEONE IN WHOM YOU HAVE NO INTEREST. WHY PERPETUATE THE PAIN?

How would you hope to have a fruitful and long-term relationship with an advisor unless you respected and trusted each other? *Your relationship must be frank, genuine, and honest.* You need to know that everything discussed is strictly confidential. You want to get to a place where you are absolutely certain that your advisor is worthy of your trust and that your interests will come first. As you have more and more interactions, your comfort level will tend to grow. Ideally, the advisor will develop a deep and long-lasting relationship with your entire family.

That takes time. Goodwill develops when the advisor becomes part of your life, through good times and difficult times. I danced at one client's wedding and then, years later, was offering advice to the couple regarding their finances as they divorced. I am there for my clients for the duration, and we share life-changing events. My dad would say, "It is the right thing to do."

One would never and should never attend a client's family event with the idea of gaining a new client, although sometimes it just happens. Some years ago, I was attending a military funeral, paying respect to one of my favorite clients. I sincerely valued his friendship and was deeply saddened to be attending his funeral. Imagine my surprise when the client's daughter asked for my business card.

Your advisor should be there to advise and consult with you in the important times of your life. That's when you know that the chemistry is right. However, sometimes, no matter what I did, I could not get the chemistry to work.

NOT READY FOR PRIME TIME

In 1985 I was an eager stockbroker, and I was given the opportunity to try to keep a client at my firm after his broker had retired.

The retiring broker's book of accounts was distributed by the branch supervisor, and I managed to book an *appointment with Mr. Big. The value of this account was a little more than $100,000. This account was twice the size of my average account at the time.*

The day of the meeting, I put on my best suit, white shirt, and new tie and headed to the meeting. I was ushered into an office that screamed, "I am an important multimillionaire." I looked around the office. Mr. Big sat at a Queen Anne desk that was magnificent. Rich tapestries hung on the walls, complementing an exquisite hand-woven rug.

He stood up to greet me. I was awestruck. He was dressed like a model on the cover of Gentlemen's Quarterly. *He could have given Dean Martin a run for his money. His shoes were shined to a blinding glow. They must have cost as much as the rent on my DC apartment. His expensive belt coordinated perfectly with his shoes. His trousers and sport jacket must have cost $3,000. He was wearing my entire bank balance.*

I was embarrassed to be in his presence, yet I put on my best stockbroker face and explained why I was there.

During the 15 minutes I spent with him, it became evident to me, even as I tried my best, that we were not connecting on any level. I was able to establish no commonality. I was not necessary or relevant to him or his world. He ushered me out and said something to the effect that we would be in touch.

I left feeling like the kid who parks your car at a fancy restaurant. I was irrelevant. As I left the building, I headed toward a nearby park and sat down to review what had just happened. I had established no rapport whatsoever. He had viewed me as an eager salesman, not as the knowledgeable advisor I was training to be. I clearly was not ready for prime time.

Fate wasn't done with me that day, not by a long shot. I passed by a bookstore on the way back to the office. Being a book lover, I looked through the window at all the titles, not in any rush to go back to work. I saw a little yellow book in the corner by someone named Dale Carnegie. The cover read, How to Win Friends and Influence People.

I looked through the window at all the titles, not in any rush to go back to work. I saw a book in the corner by someone named Dale Carnegie. The cover read, How to Win Friends and Influence People.

I muttered to myself that I needed to read that book. My chosen profession might depend on it. I went into the bookstore and got the last copy off the shelf. I devoured its lessons over the next several weeks and ultimately enrolled in a Dale Carnegie course taught in Washington.

I excelled in the course work and earned the most prestigious award, an engraved mechanical pencil. At the time, this was a very big deal. I learned and grew as a result of that book and the course. I think everyone involved in giving advice toe to toe and nose to nose should at least read the second greatest book ever written.

Were I ever to get the opportunity to meet Mr. Big again, I think I would at least have a shot at winning his favor. ◯

CHAPTER 5

A BROKER OF RELATIONSHIPS

"PRESENCE IS MORE THAN JUST BEING THERE."

MALCOLM FORBES

No relationship is one sided. You can't expect one person to do all of the work. You have to do your part as well. Remember the old saw that you get out what you put in. A relationship with your financial advisor is no different.

Suppose you were to call your advisor on Monday and were to leave a message for her to call you. It is now Thursday and still no word. How would you feel? Annoyed, and rightfully so.

Now reverse the situation. Your advisor left a message on your answering machine on Monday to call back regarding an issue with your IRA account. Again, it is now Thursday. You still have not returned her call. You tell yourself that you were busy and couldn't get around to it. But from you advisor's perspective, you haven't acted to resolve this important issue.

If this advisor were like me, he or she would have taken the time to retrieve the needed documents and review them before calling you. Now that task must be repeated. Not a particularly good use of an advisor's time.

Reflect for a moment: How did you make that advisor feel by not returning her call within a reasonable period of time? Did you strengthen the relationship? Did you help forge bonds of trust? My guess is that the relationship was weakened a notch.

I have encountered investors during my career who blamed others for just about everything and took no responsibility for a negative outcome. Many times, I could trace much of the problem back to a lack of communication. For that reason, long ago, I structured my practice so that I was responsible for a touch point every three to five weeks. I defined that as a personal phone call, e-mail, or written correspondence that I would initiate. *I firmly believe that you do not forge bonds of steel by having two interactions each year.*

I have a thick hide. I don't get easily offended if I do not receive a call back. I just call again. After I understood that much misery can be remedied by simply talking to others, I made it my point never to be a stranger to the families that I served. I created a schedule listing those I had to call each week. I would check off the name of the person I had called, take notes on the outcome, and place that person back on the schedule to begin the process again in three to five weeks.

The strangest way for planners to run an advisory business is to avoid clients. That is sheer lunacy. I doubt they teach that at Wharton or the Harvard Business School. In reading industry publications over the years, I have seen it mentioned time and time again that the main reason an advisor loses a client is not due to lack of performance; it is due to lack of communication. Communication is at the heart of any advisory relationship.

There must be open, honest, and frequent discussions if the alliance between you and your advisor is to flourish and strengthen. I decided long ago that I would never lose a client due to lack of communication.

A TEAM ON YOUR SIDE

When you have an effective relationship, you are gaining your advisor's expertise, yet remaining in control of your own financial destiny.

However, nobody, no matter how intelligent and experienced, can know it all. The best advisors place a virtual team around them to call on for expertise in various situations. I would hope that your advisor would be mindful of his or her own limitations and skills. Personally, I would not consider advising a client on setting up a particular kind of trust; I would defer instead to a credentialed expert in that area. I am not an attorney, and hence, I do not practice law.

If your financial situation dictates insurance planning and having a balanced investment portfolio, perhaps your advisor is not an expert in either category. The advisor should be able to call on experts either within the firm or affiliated with it in some manner. Over time, the complexity of wealth management has grown beyond the scope of any single person. People you may want on your team may be your financial advisor, CPA, elder-care attorney, estate-planning attorney, and perhaps an insurance specialist. Many advisory teams have access to just such expertise.

One of my colleagues summed it up quite well. He said, "We harness the intellectual capital of the entire franchise and deliver unique solutions to the families we serve." Another way of saying that is, "I don't have all the answers, but I know who does."

THE MOST EFFECTIVE ADVISORS ARE AT THEIR
BEST WHEN THEY CAN GET THAT TEAM AROUND THE
TABLE AND EVERYONE IS COMMUNICATING.

When I am meeting with a new client and I begin to understand the scope of everything involved, I, in effect, become a broker of relationships. I suggest when we could bring in other advisors to sit around a table and collaborate on strategies and solutions.

The most effective advisors are at their best when they can get that team around the table and everyone is communicating. That is how you get a coordinated strategy working for your best interests. Your advisor is the glue that holds such a team of specialists together during those times when you decide that it is necessary to call them in.

"Don't confuse activity with progress. Noise does not mean you should alter strategies that you have put in place. Just because a government official's comments have been picked up by the media does not mean you have to react at all. Rather, discuss it with your financial advisor. Odds are, your long-term goals have not changed."

Rick Rath, investment industry expert

THE NATURE OF RELATIONSHIPS

People form relationships with people. I'm convinced they do not form them with corporations. Yes, I like my Firestone tires because they hug the road and help keep my family safe. And I shop at Giant Food because it's convenient, I can find things easily, and it has good prices. But I do not have a relationship with Firestone or Giant Food.

However, I have a relationship with Scott, the manager at the tire store who sold me my Firestone tires. I have had my cars serviced there for over 15 years and have bought many tires.

George is the manager of the local Giant Food Store. He greets me whenever I come in, knows my name, knows everything in the store and where it is, and is always helpful. He always has a smile on his face.

By contrast, I cannot put a face to my Apple laptop. I like it for its ease of use, but no human relationship represents the company for me. I never had an opportunity to develop one because I bought my computer online.

My point is I have formed relationships with the people who take care of me at those stores. When they are helpful, answer my questions, guide me to make smart buying decisions, and are kind and thoughtful, I form a personal relationship with them. I benefit from their knowledge, opinions, and guidance. I have trust and confidence in them and their advice. I look forward to seeing them when I shop in their stores.

I buy gas for my car at Exxon Mobil. If it is closed, I go across the street to Chevron. My car does not care which gas I use, and neither do I. I swipe my credit card at the pump, and my car keeps driving me around town. Personal relationship? No. When was the last time an attendant at the gas station came out, greeted and assisted you, and wiped your windshield clean?

You have a relationship with your financial advisor—a good one, I hope, or a great one. The bond may be built on any number of things: shared experience, years working together, similar investment philosophy, intellectual compatibility, or admiration for the thoughtful manner the advisor has displayed in watching out for your family's best interest.

The advisor has been attentive to your needs, maybe made you a boatload of money or met with your children to help them make better financial decisions. However it took hold, perhaps the relationship developed into a true friendship. That's something you share with a person, not with the corporation that owns the desk upon which the computer sits.

I said it before, and I will say it again, the finest planners and advisors I have ever met have a passion for what they do. The families that they serve derive an immense benefit from the advisors who have a love for their craft and a constant drive to improve their skills.

You will wish to consider, when appropriate, giving referrals or introductions to your advisor *because there are people you care about and you want their interests to be looked after as carefully and as attentively as yours.*

SOMETHING LOST

With so many mergers and name changes, the corporate icons that we have known for decades have changed. In the last several years, since the financial crisis, they changed again. Many wealth management firms are now owned by insurance companies and banks. Some still have the autonomy to serve their clients as they did in the past, and some don't.

When I talk to advisors who have made the huge decision to move from one firm to another, the biggest reason I hear is that the whole culture that they knew and felt comfortable with is gone. It all changed. The personal relationships, the way of doing things, sometimes built over decades, gone.

These advisors move to a new firm, hoping to take you, the client, with them. Your relationship was with the advisor, the Richard or the Mike or the Mary Ann. It was not with the big corporation. The big corporation did not spend two hours with you and your spouse explaining important aspects of your comprehensive financial plan, drafted just for you.

The big corporation did not meet with your estate-planning attorney, your CPA, and you to coordinate the creation and placement of an insurance policy in a new life insurance trust to benefit your children and grandchildren. The big corporation did not spend hour after hour drafting a retirement income plan that gives confidence.

Oh, and the big corporation did not call to wish you a great day on your sixty-first birthday. My guess is these efforts were undertaken by the Mary Anns and the Mikes and the Richards. Such personal relationships are caring, heartfelt, and intensely human.

You do not want a servant, an order taker, or a footman as your financial consultant. You can call 1-800-trade-a-stock if you want blind obedience.

WAS THIS WHAT YOU HAD IN MIND?

You do not want a servant, an order taker, or a footman as your financial consultant. You can call 1-800-trade-a-stock if you want blind obedience. You can get someone who will follow your orders and take no interest in you or make any diligent attempt to keep you from blowing yourself up.

Let us take a look and see what the absence of a trusting relationship looks like in this hypothetical interaction with Martha and her advisor, Rick.

> Martha: Hi, Rick. I want to build out my portfolio a bit more and diversify. I need to make some trades today. Get a pencil.
>
> Rick: Oh, yeah. Hi. Okay. I'm ready.

Martha: I have a bunch of low-priced stocks I want to buy in my IRA, and I want a big discount. Okay. Buy 2,000 shares of North American Flapjack at the market. Buy 4,000 shares of Indiana Tuna and Cod, 1,000 shares of Indoor Campfires of Hoboken, and 10,000 shares of Northwest Gold and Honey. I want you to call me back immediately after they're executed and give me all of the prices and commissions. Just so you're aware, I'm executing these trades with my other fella as well, and your prices better be in line, or else. Oh, and I want you to keep sending all of the research on muni bonds too. I'm buying my bonds over at Allied Company, but I find your research easier to understand.

Rick: Okay. Let me make sure I got it all. That was...

Martha: Just get it all done and call me back as soon as possible.

Click.

Would you call this a relationship? I call it anxiety provoking. Did you see trust, knowledge, or care from either of them? Rick could not get in a word, and Martha had one demand after another. Not one *please* or *thank-you* passed their lips. Rick is an order taker and most likely afraid of his own shadow. If Rick had any sense, he would fire Martha as a client. Odds are he needs her business, even with the discounting he does for her. Why else would he allow himself to be treated that way?

And the worst part? He now has to call her back and talk to her a second time in one day.

BE OPEN TO INFLUENCE

Nick Murray, in his book *The Game of Numbers*, states: "The dominant determinant of lifetime investment outcomes is not investment performance, but investment behavior." I like to think that effective financial advisors influence the behavior of their clients, much as my coach, Brian, influences my behavior in the gym.

If your advisor periodically cautions you not to follow a particular investment strategy, he or she is trying to modify your investment behavior for a reason. Perhaps it is to steer you clear of a very risky action. By nudging you along a path, asking questions, discussing your goals and engaging with you in meaningful dialogue, the advisor shares the benefits of knowledge and experience with you.

BY NUDGING YOU ALONG A PATH, ASKING QUESTIONS, DISCUSSING YOUR GOALS AND ENGAGING WITH YOU IN MEANINGFUL DIALOGUE, THE ADVISOR SHARES THE BENEFITS OF KNOWLEDGE AND EXPERIENCE WITH YOU.

Your advisor's discovery process is ongoing; it *never* stops. It is present in periodic advisory meetings, performance reviews, and retirement and legacy planning discussions.

Effective advisors wish to keep learning about the motivations of the people they serve. The more they understand, the better they can assist and guide.

In return, what can you do to improve your relationship with your financial advisor? You can engage in meaningful conversations and allow the advisor to influence your behavior to help you attain your objectives. Stop procrastinating and begin now.

The best advisors are client focused. They exhibit compassion, empathy, and humility. These characteristics are necessary to establish the connections that forge the bonds of trust. You as the client must be able to feel comfortable in discussing and disclosing things you have probably never told anyone else.

THE RIPPLE EFFECT

The decisions that you and your advisor make may have a ripple effect, as from a pebble tossed into a pond. Those ripples will be felt by you and your family members for years and even decades to come. A wise advisor can touch your family in many meaningful ways, educating and influencing. The effect can prove to be enormous in the lives of your children or grandchildren. By creating a legacy for your family now, you may help insure that money is passed on to generations in the future.

> I HAVE WITNESSED PRUDENTLY CHOSEN INVEST-
> MENTS MULTIPLY TIME AND TIME AGAIN TO BECOME
> EXTRAORDINARILY LARGE SUMS OF MONEY
> PASSED ON TO FUTURE GENERATIONS.

Allow and encourage your financial advisor to focus on your family. Remember, the relationship is not only about cash management, stocks, bonds, or real estate. Grown children often face challenges in which the specialized knowledge of an effective financial advisor can be very helpful. It can be a good idea to invite your children to lunch or dinner with your advisor to get acquainted. Your advisor can then follow up to reassure them that they have a resource and sounding board.

This is value added to you and your family. This comes from a personal relationship, not from the World Wide Web or a magazine.

FOUR GENERATIONS STRONG

I met Stanley over 20 years ago. Over a period of years, we created a diversified portfolio to support his objec-

tives of capital growth. While Stanley and I collaborated on portfolio design, his wife, Anna, was busy at home raising their two boys and holding down a job at a local art supply store. Anna loved to sketch scenes of the water. She grew up near a beach and spent her free time as a kid sketching boats, rocky shores, docks, and kids.

Stanley was a draftsman at an architectural design firm. He loved being involved in the many details of his portfolio and investments. This was his passion. He loved to debate the merits of purchasing one stock or another.

Stanley introduced me to his mother, Sophie, after she had a bad experience with her advisor. Sophie and I met several times to discuss and review what she was trying to accomplish with her portfolio and to determine whether I could be of help. I took on the responsibility of managing her portfolio as well.

Sophie passed away several years later and left all of her assets to Stanley, her only son. I enjoyed working with Stanley and Anna and felt intellectually challenged in our many discussions. However, over time, it occurred to me that I took my relationship with Anna for granted and did not seek to actively involve her in discussions. I recognized my mistake.

I felt this was a serious lack of judgment on my part, and I worked to correct that. We soon became comfortable working together. Some years later, Stanley had a massive stroke and became a shadow of his former self. He would sit at home in a darkened living room, watching TV. He attempted as best he could to participate in discussions, but it was clear that Anna had to step into his shoes regarding many of the financial decisions.

At first, it felt strange to have financial discussion only with Anna, but each discussion built upon another, and we worked well together. The kids went off to college, and within two years, Stanley passed away and I was working exclusively with Anna. A strong mother, she provided wonderful guidance to her sons and kept the family together.

Fast forward several years. Danny, the youngest, became a copywriter and married his childhood sweetheart. Troy, the oldest, entered the Marines and became an officer with a bright future. He married, and today I am working with him and his wife in planning for the college education of their two children.

I cannot begin to express the gratitude I feel in being able to be a trusted family advisor to four generations of this family. How many professions give you the opportunity to develop such enduring relationships so that you can assist a family in such a manner? ○

CHAPTER 6

∞

WHAT'S ON YOUR MIND?

"INTEGRITY IS THE ESSENCE OF
EVERYTHING SUCCESSFUL."

R. BUCKMINSTER FULLER

O ver two decades ago, Mimi and Fred, a wonderful, life-of-the-party couple from Florida, had invested in a real estate limited partnership that invested in urban office buildings. The investment was sizable, and they looked forward to many years of dependable distributions to supplement their income in retirement. This was an illiquid investment and could not be sold.

The value of the investment multiplied significantly as did their income. It was one of the most successful investments that Mimi and Fred had ever made. Fred traded up his Pontiac to a Cadillac and then a top-of-the-line Lexus. They enjoyed good health, lived the good life and showered their three kids with unexpected gifts—a $5,000 check for

Christmas, a family cruise, and so on. They assisted their children by regularly contributing regularly to their grand-children's college funds. As the years went by, they slowed down a bit but still took an active interest in their kids, grandkids, friends, and investments.

Fred had begun to share with his advisor that, from time to time, he would receive notifications of retiring general partners and future plans to either sell the buildings, or convert the partnership to a publicly traded security. Finally, they received a letter explaining that many alternative plans were being reviewed and all of the investors would shortly be asked to vote on a final plan. Fred received a very large envelope of documents. He was asked to review the plans and to vote to convert the real estate partnership to a publicly traded, real-estate investment trust, or REIT. In the coming months, the plans received overwhelming approval.

Eventually, the real-estate investment trust went public, and Mimi and Fred were swamped with dozens of mailings informing them that electronic book entry accounts had been set up for them with a bank custodian to hold the exchanged partnership units. Fred shared these notifications with his advisor, and it quickly became evident that there was a tremendous amount of paperwork involved.

Fred's advisor listened and understood that he was overwhelmed by it all. Fred had just turned 78, and this was getting to him. He did not know what had to be done. Several times, he called an 800 number that had been provided to him, but after a long time on hold, he hung up in frustration.

Fred's advisor asked him what outcome he would like to see with all of these book entry shares in the various bank custodian accounts. "If I could wave a magic wand and make it easy," his advisor said, "tell me what it would look like to you."

Fred thought for a moment and said he would just like half of the shares deposited in his trust and half in Mimi's trust that his advisor was supervising. He asked his advisor if he could make that happen. He was expecting a no.

"Yes, we can," his advisor said.

I like to think of advisors as enablers. I expect that there are a number of financial issues that you have not shared with your advisor. My guess is that your advisor would be able to solve or assist with a number of them quite easily, if you only were to ask.

I EXPECT THAT THERE ARE A NUMBER OF FINANCIAL ISSUES THAT YOU HAVE NOT SHARED WITH YOUR ADVISOR. MY GUESS IS THAT YOUR ADVISOR WOULD BE ABLE TO SOLVE OR ASSIST WITH A NUMBER OF THEM QUITE EASILY, IF YOU ONLY WERE TO ASK.

As for Fred, a little more than 90 days later, the book entry accounts were closed. Half of the shares were now held in each of their trusts, and the stress was gone from Fred's face and voice. His advisor was able to assist him and Mimi and remove a great deal of frustration from their financial lives.

SORTING OUT YOUR CONCERNS

An effective financial advisor will help you sort out what's on your mind. I ask my clients, "Do you have any questions for me today?" I want to make sure that we put on the table and explore anything that they have been thinking about, that they were saving up to ask me. Have this type of discussion with your advisor.

Such thoughts might occur to you as you read the paper, watch a commercial, or chat with your dentist. "I never thought of establishing a minimum level of income in retirement," you might think. "I've always relied on dividends, but those can go up or down. Maybe I'd have more confidence if my income wasn't tied to the markets."

Get those matters out on the table, and discuss them with your advisor. I often have found that when I ask my clients open-ended questions, great things begin to happen: "What's on your mind? Are there any *issues, concerns, or questions* that you would like to discuss with me?"

HEARING WHAT NEEDS TO BE SAID

A committed and insightful financial advisor will also figure out what is not being said. When you look into people's eyes as they talk with you, sometimes you sense that you are hearing a partial truth, that something is hidden behind the curtain.

WHEN YOU LOOK INTO PEOPLE'S EYES AS THEY
TALK WITH YOU, SOMETIMES YOU SENSE THAT
YOU ARE HEARING A PARTIAL TRUTH, THAT
SOMETHING IS HIDDEN BEHIND THE CURTAIN.

"You might have concerns," I will ask. "Is there anything that you think I should be aware of that will affect you financially?" The key part of that is "that I should be aware of." For example, perhaps a client is requesting more funds than normal and I find out that a child is in a rehab facility. Some issues are very private, yet once we understand that the client needs access to more money, we can look for ways to adjust the portfolio.

There are times when an advisor has to get up and close the office door. Advisors hear things that people won't tell anyone else. We hear about substance abuse, gambling problems, financial blunders. The very best financial advisors, I believe, are part therapists, psychologists, and trusted confidants. Listening is an art, and it must be practiced. Clients' emotions often pour out. A good advisor knows to keep a box of tissues nearby.

EFFICIENCY AND EFFECTIVENESS GO HAND IN HAND

To be efficient in my practice, I must work from a well-thought-out list of items that must be accomplished. I prioritize those items, and I tackle the most important and difficult ones first. That's in keeping with Brian Tracy's advice in his book *Eat That Frog!*: If you were to start your day by eating the biggest, ugliest frog you could find, everything else that day would seem simple.

Tracy emphasized the importance of "thinking on paper," the way my dad did years ago at the laundry, when he pulled out his pencil and yellow pad. The most effective advisors and consultants will have all of your action items on paper or on a spreadsheet as well. They would not dream of leaving your financial security to their memory.

When your advisor is mapping out a strategy for you, there will be many moving parts, some simple and some more complex. Plans are drafted, corrected, and redrafted until the kinks are worked out. *To be effective, your advisor must tackle the most critical items first and make sure every aspect of your plan is executed properly.* The best advisors I have met take a global view of a client's situation and then work to ensure that each issue is methodically addressed according to its importance.

I have witnessed practices where no one person on a team was responsible and, as a result, very little was accomplished. They seemed to be going around and around, asking if this or that was accomplished, with no one person answerable for anything. This, of course, would lead to one delay after another, one correction after another. The end result was sloppy, due to poor execution. As important as it is for consultants and advisors to be skillful and responsible, it is critical that they surround themselves with a staff that is capable of thorough work and meticulous follow-up.

A MATTER OF PRIORITIES

Whether your time is spent babysitting grandkids or on the golf course, you do not want to be involved in endless discussions with your advisor and his or her staff on trivial manners. You and your advisor must set priorities. Make sure they don't look different to you than they do to your advisor. You need to be on the same page.

Take the situation where I was asked to examine the investments of an ill and elderly relative of someone I knew. The person who requested my assistance held the power of attorney for the sick relative and was rightly concerned that the assets, whatever they were, were on autopilot with no one monitoring them. I reviewed each of the account statements provided. Although I was not thrilled with what I saw, I knew that the deeper problem was whether this individual had set up an estate or legacy plan, especially because he had just moved from one state to another to be closer to his family.

As it turned out, the sole legal document in place was the power of attorney—no will, or health-care directives, and so on. I knew this was the priority, not the monthly statement. I put them in touch with someone who could assist them in the planning process. When that was completed, I recommended a few minor adjustments to increase liquid cash reserves. Efficiency goes hand in hand with effectiveness; it is essential to know what to do and what order to do it in. ○

THE POWER OF THE PROCESS

I would expect that your consultant or advisory team has discussed a process with you. This is the structure, discipline, and strategy to get you to where you want to be. Spend time to understand the strategy crafted for you. Be on guard for any signs that the advisor is winging it. A professional, whether a wealth management advisor, a retirement advisor, or financial planner, should have a clearly articulated plan that you can understand.

Over the years, I've met many highly intelligent solo practitioners, as well as advisors who are part of a team. Some were affiliated with large insurance groups or brokerage companies. You never know where you will find great people, which is why I never rule out any group. Some people have developed their own planning strategies. Others use the resources of large firms. There is more than one road to excellence, and I have found that many paths can take you there.

Look for well-conceived, thoughtful solutions that showcase a reasonable approach, considering your objectives. If the strategy cannot be explained to you so that you can then recite back the salient points to your advisor, you need to stop and consider if this makes sense for you. Look at the advisor's diagnostic process. Does it seem well thought out?

Over the years, I have offered a second-opinion service in which I examine statements for clients, friends, and family. I have found portfolios overwhelmingly overweighted to a single asset class, such as real-estate securities, annuities, or growth stocks. I could be politically correct and say that the portfolios were a bit lopsided, or I could express myself like the native New Yorker I am and say, *"Who the heck built this portfolio?"* However the solutions are delivered to you, look for the strategy behind them. If it doesn't make sense, question it.

For example, I am a nut about liquidity. Long ago I heard the phrase "access to cash without pain." It has become my mantra. I have heard comments such as these, as people tell me how they manage their cash needs: "Oh, if I need additional cash, I can always sell one of my stocks at a profit." But in a down market? Or they may say, "If I'm short of funds, I can sell put options on a stock that I own." Some even maintain that there is no such thing as an unforeseen need for cash.

I would reply that holding a portion of your portfolio in cash reserves is prudent. We all have experienced expenses we hadn't known were coming. I would say that qualifies as an unforeseen need for cash. For example, my wife, Reena, calls me at the office and informs me that a big part of our air-conditioning system needs to be replaced, for $4,800. Or she may tell me that her car died and her mechanic said it made more sense to buy a new one. There are excellent reasons to have a robust cash reserve, and I'm sure you can think of even more compelling examples than mine.

Financial advisors are expected to be knowledgeable about a wide array of investments and planning strategies. They must be able to share these with you in a manner that is helpful and not condescending. The advisors who have impressed me the most over the course of my career share many of the following traits:

thoughtful	observant	results oriented
reliable	patient	long-term perspective
attentive	effective	trustworthy
polite	organized	insightful
skilled	efficient	dependable
methodical	ambitious	intelligent
empathetic	focused	capable
vigilant	genuine	caring

Read through the list again. Do some of these characteristics describe your advisor? I hope so. People who possess these traits in abundance are a rare catch.

TRUTHFULNESS IS ESSENTIAL

When you are dealing with your advisor, you need to be open and forthcoming. Your goal should be to build a meaningful and respectful relationship over time. That happens by treating your advisor as you would wish to be treated. It's a fundamental of relationships that most people learn in childhood.

Sometimes a client fails to disclose something important in my discovery process. I tend to think this sort of thing is an oversight, rather than intentional. If you entered a relationship with an advisor and didn't disclose important information, you need to examine why you have done this. What did you hope to accomplish by withholding needed facts about your situation?

I CANNOT UNDERSTAND WHY YOU WOULD ASK SOMEONE FOR PROFESSIONAL GUIDANCE AND THEN NOT PROVIDE ALL OF THE NECESSARY INFORMATION. YOUR ADVISOR NEEDS FULL DISCLOSURE TO DO THE BEST JOB POSSIBLE FOR YOU.

In discussions with advisors, I am told that some clients seem to think there's something to be gained by keeping the advisor in the dark. I cannot understand why you would ask someone for professional guidance and then not provide all of the necessary information. Your advisor needs full disclosure to do the best job possible for you.

NO ROOM FOR BAD ATTITUDES

Trust is a two-way street, and we all have a bad day once in a while and are not always in the best of spirits. I know that if I call a client while I'm in such a mood, my negative feelings seem to travel right through those phone wires, and the person on the other end picks that up. The call is not successful, and it should never have been made. My simple remedy: I take some deep breaths, smile, think of how I am going to help this person, and then pick up the phone for a meaningful conversation.

I recognize that your advisor might call you when you're having a bad day. As I've just mentioned, your attitude will come through the phone, and the advisor might be thinking, "What did I do wrong? What did I say? What did I do that was annoying?" For both advisor and client, it's helpful to say, "You haven't caught me at a good time. Perhaps we could talk at another time when I'm not so stressed."

I believe that an experienced financial consultant should never accept a new client who offers only a modest portion of his or her portfolio for the advisor to manage. What is the intent there? To see whether the advisor does a good job for four quarters before getting any more to manage? The advisor would wonder, "Is this a race? Do I have to prove myself against some other account before I'm deemed worthy?" Some clients look at a popular financial index to gauge how they should be doing. I firmly believe that a 73-year-old, married, retired couple should not be benchmarking the performance of their retirement portfolio against an index that may be up 26 percent in one year and down 17 percent in the next.

Clients need to embrace the idea that advisors are professionals. They're not there to beat the index. Advisors are there to counsel you, to work with you, and to be truthful, honest, and forthright in trying to assist you to get to your goals.

CLIENTS NEED TO EMBRACE THE IDEA THAT ADVISORS ARE PROFESSIONALS. THEY'RE NOT THERE TO BEAT AN INDEX. ADVISORS ARE THERE TO COUNSEL YOU, TO WORK WITH YOU, AND TO BE TRUTHFUL, HONEST, AND FORTHRIGHT.

For example, if a couple in their late 60s were to invest $2 million or even $4 million with an advisor, what is their objective? What do they want? Is it to earn a 24 percent rate of return, or is it to have the money invested wisely in accordance with their goals and objectives, tolerance for risk, and cash flow needs, or is it, perhaps, to earn a reasonable rate of return over and above taxes and inflation?

Most advisors are not in the business of beating an arbitrary index. They are in the business of helping people solve problems, such as ensuring adequate income in retirement, providing an intelligently thought-out legacy for the children, or effectively planning a college fund.

INSISTING ON CONSISTENCY

People develop trust with others over time when there is a familiar consistency in words and deeds. The interactions with your advisor should have an air of consistency. Many investors are grateful that this is the type of relationship that they enjoy with their financial advisor. Some still search for that kind of relationship. How would you interpret your advisor's behavior or intentions if you saw an investment philosophy that changed year to year or meeting to meeting? You want to see actions that are in harmony with past conversations and strategies.

Sally Hogshead, in her book *Fascinate: Your 7 Triggers to Persuasion and Captivation*, wrote, "The more people trust what they're being told, and the more they trust the person giving them this information, the more likely they are to follow it."

What would you think if your advisor continually made it clear that you should not speculate with aggressive stocks in your IRA account and then began recommending exactly that? Or if you had been counseled to never buy securities with borrowed money, using a margin account, and then your advisor pushed you to pursue that same strategy?

Watch for cues or signposts that may signify a change of attitude, philosophy, or strategies. Such changes need to be brought out into the open and discussed in depth.

HOW YOU REALLY FEEL ABOUT MONEY

At some point, as you are developing a bond with your advisor so that you can share what is important, you should talk about your innermost feelings and fears about money. In other words, *what does money mean to you?* This could either be the silliest question you ever heard or the best.

You will be digging up long-suppressed money emotions, such as fears of not having enough, losing what you have, or taking too much risk. The emotions carried with these thoughts are visceral. You can feel goose bumps. Help your advisor really understand what risk means to you. Is it, perhaps, not having enough resources to assist your kids, your parents, or your grandkids?

This has nothing to do with financial ratios, graphs and charts, standard deviation, or beta. This is where your financial advisor understands your money personality. Share your memories of how you grew up with money, what loss means to you, what risk means to you. The connections you establish with your advisor must be real and intentional. They must be forged, and sharing the core of how you perceive money will go a long way toward establishing bonds of steel.

All investors, at some level, have fears in regard to their money. You, as an investor, must be aware of your own fears and be able to communicate them to your advisor. Yes, it's very personal. Yes, it may be embarrassing or downright illogical, but they are your fears.

A common fear of retirees is running out of money and having to go back to work. I visit department stores and notice elderly greeters at the door. I suspect that was not their vision of retirement. On those rare occasions when I visit a fast-food restaurant, I have sometimes given my order to someone old enough to be my dad.

There are no rights or wrongs here. It simply is what it is. We all have quirks in our personality when it comes to money. What's yours? Make sure your financial advisor is in the loop. As a result, he or she will be able to serve your interests better, and those of your family. By understanding what drives you and what might hold you back, the advisor can offer you the solutions that fit you best. You will have created another link in the bond of trust.

CHAPTER 7

ALL IN THE FAMILY

*"SUCCESS IS DOING ORDINARY
THINGS EXTRAORDINARILY WELL."*

JIM ROHN

Years ago, I dealt with the successful owner of a manufacturing facility on the East Coast. He had two sons, neither of whom had any interest in the business. Although he would liked to have kept the business that he had spent decades building in the family, it was not meant to be.

The eldest son wanted to become an eye surgeon and the youngest, a geologist. My client shared with me that he intended to finance both their undergraduate and graduate school costs out of cash flow, and that doing this was not a concern.

Over the years, he purchased cars and homes for them. The boys came to expect that this was how it was in their family—no need to contribute sweat, equity, or dollars. "Dad will pay," they figured. "We've got college paid for. We've got grad school paid for, cars, and a home. The best part is we have no debt." This illustrates what I call the law of unintended consequences.

The boys' mother died in an auto accident, and now it was just them and their dad. Communication between them became infrequent. When I met with this man, I was stunned to learn that the boys and he no longer spoke to each other.

Fast forward. The boys are successful in their chosen fields, and they have started families of their own, far from the East Coast. Their dad is not a part of his grandchildren's lives.

I am not privy to the discussions that went on inside their four walls, but I can tell you this. I believe that the boys' lives were made too easy and that they were not taught that you need skin in the game. Sometimes parents do harm in trying to help their kids. My friend Richard Watts writes about this extensively in his wonderful book *Fables of Fortune: What Rich People Have That You Don't Want.*

Their dad gave them everything they could ask for and more, but what he gave most was money. Could he have given more of himself and less of the cash? Perhaps. What did he end up getting? Something he had never even considered: a poor family situation, built upon generosity.

MORE HARM THAN GOOD

That story demonstrates that you need to plan how you're going to treat your kids, especially when there is family money. Don't think family money means millions. It does not. Family money is often measured in thousands. Besides, I have no experience in dealing with people whose net worth is measured in the hundreds of millions of dollars.

Back in the days when I helped in my dad's laundry, I had to work many hours, sweating and feeling filthy, to earn the money that I needed to buy a 10-speed bicycle. That blue beast was my prized possession for years. If it had just been given to me as a present, I don't know if I would have treated it in the same manner. Maybe, I would have been more cavalier about it. I really had skin in the game, and it meant a lot to me.

If we make it too easy for our children, we may, in fact, cause more harm than good. When passing money to the kids, parents must make sure that they pass on their values as well. This is an issue that many families face when working with their advisor.

IF WE MAKE IT TOO EASY FOR OUR CHILDREN, WE MAY, IN FACT, CAUSE MORE HARM THAN GOOD. WHEN PASSING MONEY TO THE KIDS, PARENTS MUST MAKE SURE THAT THEY PASS ON THEIR VALUES AS WELL.

FORGING BONDS OF STEEL

How to efficiently pass on money is a common consideration in retirement planning. Often the children deserve it; they have done well in their careers and would be good stewards of the money. Even so, you want to pass on your money in the most effective way. This is your legacy, and you need to take great care in passing on your money and your values.

This bears repeating: *Do not only pass on your money. Make certain that it is accompanied by your values.* I have witnessed more than my fair share of kids who have been left sizable inheritances, far greater than their ability to properly manage it. If you like, call them trust fund babies. I am not talking about the ones splashed on the front pages of magazines at the grocery store checkout counter. I'm talking about the deceased parents who owned an insurance agency in New Jersey and who now have a daughter who has not worked an honest day in her life. Or the son who has had four homes and has four ex-wives, but has never had a real job as that's for regular people. These children are now dysfunctional, and it's not all their fault.

Trust fund babies can be hurt for life. This needs to be a serious consideration on your part. It can be a huge mistake to provide unrestricted access to a young person with little or no financial experience. Many of these situations can be resolved through effective legacy planning with a qualified attorney. I am not an estate attorney, but I know many of them, and I have great working relationships with them. My own attorney has completed effective planning for my family situation, and I feel very comfortable that it is now in place. You see, I practice what I preach.

AN ATTORNEY'S WISDOM

I had the good fortune of meeting Richard Watts, an attorney and author from California, while he was traveling through the Washington area promoting his book *Fables of Fortune: What Rich People Have That You Don't Want.* I participated in an evening-with-the-author discussion, and he had his audience captivated with stories of the financial mistakes that very wealthy families make. Watts is an advisor to some of the richest families in America.

He spoke of the unavoidable complications that money can bring to families and, ultimately, the unintentional harm done to children who receive unrestricted access to large sums of money. This is especially true before those children achieve the level of emotional and financial maturity needed to deal with the newfound wealth in a manner that's productive and not harmful.

One of the takeaways from Watts' talk was that it's not only wealthy families that make huge monetary mistakes with their kids. It also happens to families without million-dollar estates. His message is vitally important to many.

Here's how Richard Watts explains it in his book:

> *Can you imagine the lessons lost when a youth is given a job at the family company or inherits millions of dollars?*

The greatest misconception people have about wealth is believing it is a good thing to leave large sums of money to their children. Most estate planning is done under the design of top estate-planning lawyers who have one directive: pass along as much wealth to the next generation as possible, minimizing the estate tax. Few of these bright lawyers have seen the destruction this wealth creates in the downstream generations. Even small estates—say, a family home worth $400,000—can create a war between siblings, who may find themselves in court destroying all family relationships permanently. It takes only a couple of hundred thousand dollars, given without forethought, to derail one of your children in the future. Think it through carefully and discuss the various possibilities.

You would do well to pick up a copy of Richard Watts' book.

AN UNPLANNED LEGACY

Fred, a dear client, asked that I work with a friend of his who had been ill and hospitalized. I spoke with his friend Randy the next afternoon, which was a Friday.

Randy's wife, Margie, had passed away a year earlier at age 72. Randy was two years older. He told me he had meant to work on their accounts since Margie died, but never found the time and then began feeling tired and depressed.

He related that he had always been a do-it-yourself investor with brokerage and mutual fund accounts at over a dozen firms. Now he had no interest in any of it and he wanted someone to "handle everything."

He told me that all of the accounts were held jointly with his wife, and he had never changed the registrations to his single name after she passed away. Additionally, he indicated that he had not taken any action on either of their IRA accounts and had not completed their annual required minimum distributions for the last two years.

As he spoke, my mind was racing with all of the issues he had just brought up and all of the work that needed to be done. As I thought of this, he went on to mention that he did not have a will or power of attorney. In fact, Randy and Margie had done no estate or legacy planning whatsoever.

We made arrangements to sit down and talk on Monday afternoon. I started making notes on all of the issues that had to be reviewed and sat prioritizing them for the rest of the afternoon. The list went on and on.

As I drove home, I was thinking about the son he mentioned who lived a few hours away. Because Randy used a wheelchair, the son would end up doing a good portion of the work for his dad.

On Monday morning, I received a call from Fred, who had referred Randy to me. Randy had passed away the previous day in his sleep. I sat there trying to take this all in. Fred mentioned that he was like a second father to the son and cared deeply about him.

A bit more than a year later, Fred related to me the following: The son, as sole heir, had hired an attorney to work on the estate. The son had transferred the entire inheritance, approximately $1.6 million, to his local bank. He then bought a new million-dollar home. The bank was only too happy to give him a mortgage. He then bought a new luxury car. The bank was only too happy to give him a car loan. In addition, the bank is managing all of his inheritance funds. I hope he has a good advisor at the bank.

The issue that I find most disturbing is that the son dramatically changed his life, spending hundreds of thousands of dollars on impulse so shortly after burying his father. His advisor should have been able to slam the brakes on that kind of behavior, as it rarely has a good ending.

I was amazed, but sadly, it's not the first time such things have happened, nor will it be the last. Sometimes the children are acting in spite, spending money in a manner they know their parents would have disliked. When a pile of money changes hands, the recipient tends to lose sight of all those decades of hard work that went into creating it. It's not the first time a parent's dreams turned into a child's $85,000 luxury car. ○

SETTING LIMITS ON YOUR HEIRS

It need not be that way. If you are concerned that your child might be the type who would frivolously squander your legacy on a fancy car or expensive vacations, you should be aware of the many ways that you can set some guidelines and limits on how the money will be used.

Working with an experienced financial advisor and, ultimately, with an attorney and estate planning professional, you can set up trusts and other tools whereby you can control how your money is spent and ensure certain types of behavior—even after you are long gone.

YOU CAN CONTROL HOW YOUR MONEY IS SPENT AND ENSURE CERTAIN TYPES OF BEHAVIOR— EVEN AFTER YOU ARE LONG GONE.

It is a very controversial subject. Some people think it is wise. Other people say, "When I'm gone, I'm gone. It's for the kids to do as they please." You will make your own determination about how you feel and what's right for your situation. Above all, discuss it with your advisors and arrive at a well-thought-out decision.

In any family, there are likely to be some people who manage money well and some who do not. Those who manage money poorly may simply lack maturity, or maybe, they are inept by nature and never are going to have good sense. Can you trust your children to make intelligent decisions?

One of the best ways of finding that out is to know if the child feels comfortable in asking for help. The child might open up an account at an 800 number and direct everything without any guidance whatsoever. What makes you think that a child earning $48,000 a year has the wherewithal to be able to properly oversee and invest $450,000? Receiving a check for $450,000 is very different from having $12,000 in the ABC growth mutual fund.

We all know people who have blown a fortune. They've gotten some big severance or settlement and managed to spend it all on things they figured they deserved. If you have any doubts about your children, why put them in the way of temptation? It's normal to want what is best for your children. You worried about them when they were in diapers. You worried about them when they headed off to school, and you still worry about them when they too are getting gray hair. You know they need your counsel, and you can continue to provide that even when you are looking down from some higher place.

Yes, you want them to make their own decisions, but sometimes you may face a situation in which you need to limit those choices. You can do so whether you are a multimillionaire with extensive holdings or whether you have a modest nest egg to protect, perhaps a 401(k) or IRA. You can find ways to ensure that the money comes out gradually for your heirs and not as a lump sum. After all, it is your money and your responsibility. Seek advice and do not be rushed into any decision.

YOU CALL THIS RETIREMENT?

Unforeseen circumstances have the power to compromise the retirement of your dreams. A couple imagines their retirement years together and all of the things they will do. Then, one of them dies suddenly. You never know what might happen. But you can get a pretty good idea of what will happen when a sizable sum is left to someone who lacks the wherewithal to handle it.

Early in my career, I received a call from a client, late in the day on a Friday, just as I was gathering my things to leave the office. Let us call her Elizabeth. Her husband, Harvey, had just passed away that week, and she was calling to inform me.

I reflected for a moment on the last time I had met with them. They were in the DC area to visit with family. The couple had lived all their life in the Southwest and had one son in high school. Harvey was bright and charming. He had an infectious laugh and was one of the smartest fellows I have known. He was a senior-level executive in the railroad industry and had a generous defined benefit pension plan. He was close to retiring. The pension plan would ensure that Elizabeth had ample cash flow to live on.

As it turned out, their son, Austin, took his dad's death very hard. His schoolwork suffered, he quit the hockey team at school, and he kept to himself in his bedroom. He would join his mom for dinner and then retreat up to his room again, behind locked doors. Harvey had been saving and investing for Austin's college education with a Uniform Gift to Minors account invested in a variety of mutual funds. The account had grown to almost $130,000 at the time of Harvey's death.

Austin skated through the rest of his senior year in high school and graduated at the rock bottom of his class. Austin's dad had never kept it a secret from his son that he was investing for his future. On Austin's eighteenth birthday, he demanded that his mom change the account registration to his single name. He contacted me a short time later and directed that all investments in the account be liquidated and placed into a money market fund and that he be issued a check card and checkbook.

In less than eight months, Austin spent down nearly the entire amount his dad had saved and invested for his college education. Although his mom was a strong-willed scientist, she was no match for an angry, 200-pound, muscle-packed teenager. Austin bought himself two cars. He bought every kind of fancy and expensive watch he could find. He had two girlfriends to whom he gave cars as well. Both girlfriends became pregnant.

Last I heard, the kids were living with Austin's retired mother. Austin had a part-time job at a glass factory. His two ex-girlfriends were neither in school nor employed. Elizabeth is raising her two granddaughters while her son works part-time and thinks nothing of the future. Perhaps he will enroll in classes at the community college, perhaps not. Elizabeth loves her granddaughters dearly. But is this the retirement she and Harvey had dreamed about? Is this what they planned? Not by a long shot.

This was not a family with millions in assets. This was a family that had put together a $780,000 nest egg and left $130,000 to a child. This story does not involve seven figures, but it is quite enough to do damage to an *immature person who has never had many dollars in his pocket. Many children have no knowledge of money or how it works. America's schools do an exceptionally poor job of preparing our children for a future where they will interact with money every day.* ○

A GRANDMA SPURNED

From time to time I just have to scratch my head at how events play themselves out. If you wished to offer a helping hand for your grandchild's college education, I'm sure that you would discuss your wishes with your son or daughter and arrive at a plan to give a gift to be invested in some kind of college savings program.

You may consider mutual fund shares or common stocks, a CD, a Uniform Gift to Minors account, or perhaps a 529 college savings program. Regardless of how the funds are to be invested, the money is to be used as a gift for the benefit of your grandchild.

I had a client who wished to provide such a gift to her grandchild. The child's parents did not have sufficient income to put away money for college. Grandma's gift required no out-of-pocket expenses from them. My client asked me to reach out to her son-in-law to arrange some of the details of the gift.

Five weeks and four unreturned calls later, I finally got word that the son-in-law was of a mind that it was not a good idea. The program expenses were too high, he believed, although at that point no program had been chosen. In fact, we had never even engaged in a conversation.

Finally, his wife—my client's daughter—contacted me to say her husband was in charge of all investments and she was not going to interfere. In a respectful tone, I asked about their investment experience and was informed that they had a savings account, and that was about it.

I spoke to my client soon thereafter and explained that her son-in-law had spurned the gift. She was, in a word, dumbfounded. Sometimes good intentions are not enough. I suggested that we call a family meeting to explore the root causes at work there. Grandma refused my recommendation. So be it.

FAIR BUT NOT EQUAL

I have come to appreciate and embrace the idea of fair but not equal. This is controversial, so bear with me. I believe that some kids are more deserving or more in need or more responsible than others.

Let me give you an example. Suppose your son is a surgeon and very wise with money. Your daughter works in a county aide office assisting young pregnant mothers. Their economic circumstances are quite different. Does your son need to receive the same amount of inheritance as your daughter? Will your daughter need more assistance than her brother?

It may be that you will decide, during your legacy planning, that being fair does not mean you have to be equal in dollars. You may reason that your son, the surgeon, will likely create millions of dollar in assets over his lifetime, whereas your daughter, the social worker, has no hope of doing so. Perhaps your son lives on a two-acre estate with a 4,000-square-foot home and your daughter lives in a one-bedroom, rented, garden apartment. Be mindful of the possibility that "fair but not equal" may make sense in your family.

I have spoken with many people who pooh-pooh that thought and say, "No. Each of my kids gets an even share and that's just how it's got to be." There is no right or wrong decision. What's best is what you and your family feel most comfortable with.

THE MAGIC OF 4 PERCENT

Other than providing financial assets, you can leave an enduring legacy for your children by giving them the tools for success. One of the joys of doing what I do is engaging in discussions with parents on how to assist their children in being successful. Parents want their kids to succeed in life, whether in selling software, researching biochemicals, owning a boutique, selling life insurance, teaching, or becoming an entrepreneur. This type of family-related discussion tends to create strong bonds between clients and their advisors.

We discuss that it is important for their kids to learn how to allocate their time and how to prioritize what is important to them. I explain it this way: Each of us has 168 hours each week to divide up as we choose. No matter how rich or poor, thin or fat, cool or nerdy you are, you still have the same 168 hours. Last I checked, it's true in Arkansas, California, the Ukraine, and Australia. The math is simple. Twenty-four hours times seven days equals 168 hours a week. No more, no less. Imagine if they were to devote just one hour each day to the study of something—perfecting sales skills, increasing typing speed, learning to speed read, increasing computer skills, sharpening marketing skills, understanding chemistry or biology, or even learning how to write a business letter. Imagine how much better they would get.

IT IS IMPORTANT FOR THEIR KIDS TO LEARN
HOW TO ALLOCATE THEIR TIME AND HOW TO
PRIORITIZE WHAT IS IMPORTANT TO THEM.

One hour every day equates to 4.16 percent of their time. Let's just round it off to 4 percent. So, if your newly graduated son or daughter were to land a job selling widgets, and they structured their time to include one solid hour each day to increase their understanding of how the best widget professionals do it, do you think that over the course of one year they would greatly increase their widget abilities? Consider this. One hour per day for a year equals 365 hours. For those fond of the 40-hour workweek, this is the equivalent of nine full weeks of widget study—actually, 9.125 weeks.

Let's say their occupation is direct marketing of medical sales equipment. How much do you think they would benefit if they took a nine-week course in enhancing their marketing and selling skills? Would your son or daughter double or triple their knowledge, sales, confidence, and effectiveness over the course of the next year? Ponder that for a moment. What does it take? An hour of reading each day. Please note that I said, "each day." I did not say, "Take the weekend off." That is the price of success; it is not negotiable.

When I have this discussion with parents of young people in their 20s, their eyes light up. I know many young people starting out in their careers do not want to read anymore. They finished four years of college and are done with books, but they still should consider where they might fit in that one hour per day. Perhaps they could watch three football games weekly instead of four. Perhaps they could enjoy two happy hours instead of three.

My point is this: It's only 4 percent of a day, but a great return on enhancing knowledge and skills. And the other 96 percent of the day is theirs to do with as they choose. What does getting to the top of their industry take? Try 4 percent. It's magic.

RESPECTING BOTH SPOUSES

I have learned that both spouses must be involved in the planning process, even if one shows little interest. Years ago, in the 1980s, I dealt with a wife who took no interest whatsoever in any financial discussions. Shortly after her husband died, she transferred all of the assets out of my firm. I should not have been surprised, as I had done something dreadfully wrong. I had allowed the wife not to be present in any of the conversations.

If she answered the phone when I called their home, I made the mistake of asking, "Is your husband home?" I made errors in judgment and, therefore, created no bonds of trust with her whatsoever. When her husband eventually passed away, there was no reason for her to leave the funds with me and my firm because I did not have a relationship with her.

I have witnessed how offensive this can be to women and men. Some years ago, I worked with a couple who were both very successful and in the technology industry. They had three small children. The oldest was eight years old. As we worked through both the planning, insurance, and financial issues, it was evident that they had neglected to create the necessary powers of attorney, health-care directive, and wills. Also, it was clear to me that a trust for the benefit of the minor children might be appropriate, but that was for an attorney to determine.

I knew that I had to put them in touch with a local estate-planning attorney to discuss the actions that needed to be taken. I arranged a lunch at a local Italian restaurant near their home. We all sat and chatted for about 20 or 25 minutes before the food came. As we sat and talked, it was evident that the attorney was directing most of his remarks to the husband and virtually ignoring the wife. I sat there trying to figure out an intelligent way of steering the conversation to the neglected spouse—and then all hell broke loose.

The wife threw a well-deserved fit and basically told the attorney that he was a jerk. She sat there, putting him in his place like a teacher berating a 12-year-old boy for misbehaving in class. "How dare you assume that my husband makes all of the decisions in our family, you sexist jerk!" I watched as the attorney sank in his chair, trying desperately to dodge the verbal barbs. The whole event was over in less than four minutes, and I learned one of the biggest lessons in my professional career: never assume.

THE WIFE THREW A WELL-DESERVED FIT AND BASICALLY
TOLD THE ATTORNEY THAT HE WAS A JERK.

From that day on, I have taken special care to always direct my comments to both spouses, moving my eyes equally between each, never assuming who makes the decisions in the family. I hope you never have to give that kind of lecture to your advisor, attorney, or accountant.

IT'S A FAMILY AFFAIR

Your spouse or significant other needs to be involved in important decisions that involve the future. I cannot overemphasize how important it is that one spouse cannot hide in the corner. It is prudent to assure yourself that your advisor has a good working relationship with you, as well as your spouse.

Many times, the children will eventually become clients of your advisor. Of the 36 clients of mine who have died during my career, I still work with the children or beneficiaries of 33 of them, and this is after 30 years. An experienced advisor can transition smoothly to serve your spouse or other beneficiaries as well as he or she served you. The advisor might say, "William, I remember I used to talk to your dad about this, and he felt very strongly that you should never do X." The children appreciate this, and we develop a sense of continuity.

Your advisor can do more than just help your children handle your assets once you have passed away. The advisor can pass on your philosophies to them as well. That continuity is priceless.

When I was a young pup and took the Series 7 exam to be a registered representative, nobody warned me about all of the funerals and all of the death certificates that I would be working with. A large percentage of my clients are in their 60s, 70s, and 80s, many approaching the end of their lifespan.

I try to keep my clients' memories alive and to share those memories with their children. I love conversations that I have with clients' children when I tell them, "Your mom always felt strongly about this," or "Your dad always cautioned never to do that," or "Your grandfather used to tell me this story." And the children love those conversations too. There are few times in their lives when they will hear comments such as those from someone who cared about one of their family members.

PROCRASTINATION PERILS

In these pages, I have characterized advisors as facilitators and enablers. Let me go a step further and say they can force a sense of urgency.

Everyone I know procrastinates about some things in life. My son, Jason, procrastinates about cleaning his room, my colleague John, about cleaning up his desk, my business partner, Joe, about reading all of the interesting articles I tear out of magazines for him.

However, the procrastination that could really do harm to you and your family has to do with legacy planning, or, more specifically, the lack of it. The idea is to get emotionally focused on something important.

I have helped facilitate and complete the financial and legacy plans for many families. I am not a certified financial planner as is my business partner, Joe Wong, nor am I an attorney. I do not hold myself out to be either one of these. What I have done is to work side by side with people like them for decades, assisting in the creation and refinement of plans to fit each family, based on circumstances and desired outcomes. So I will say that I possess some experience in this area.

I am not an expert. I am merely an informed observer. The harm that I have witnessed is when life events occur before plans are created and in place. I have witnessed dementia, Alzheimer's disease, stroke, and other health-related issues come to pass when assets are held in the name of the person with the illness and no power of attorney or legacy-planning documents exist. From first-hand observation, I have witnessed the frustration and emotions of the family members who have to deal with attorneys and the court system.

Much of this might have been avoided with a properly drafted estate or legacy plan. This is why I try to light a fire under the families I work with to complete what I know must be completed without procrastination. I will inject a forced sense of urgency where necessary. I can become the ultimate nudge. I look out for the families involved and do not stop until they accomplish what I know they should accomplish.

I have read accounts of spouses asking that all single-name assets titled in the name of their ill spouse be transferred to them. I would inquire if they have the legal documents that would support such a move and if they have spoken to a CPA and attorney on the advisability of the action.

If the advisor gets a blank stare as a result, I think that means the request is a knee-jerk reaction to have funds available to pay nursing home expenses with no advanced planning.

A LOT MORE THAN MONEY

Even though my father died 17 years ago, I am still a co-trustee with my sister on a small trust that he created. Every day I see my dad's name as part of the financial work that I do in checking and rechecking all of the accounts and assets for which I am responsible. It is a chore I'm happy to take on. Yet it comes tied with a bundle of emotions and memories.

I love my dad dearly and I miss him. However, looking at his name every single day while I'm at work sometimes is distracting. In that way, understand how advisors feel about dealing with estate events. Financial planning and estate and legacy planning involve a lot more than money. They involve people and family, lives, traditions, and deep and sometimes unsettled emotions.

FINANCIAL PLANNING AND ESTATE AND LEGACY PLANNING INVOLVE A LOT MORE THAN MONEY. THEY INVOLVE PEOPLE AND FAMILY, LIVES, TRADITIONS, AND DEEP AND SOMETIMES UNSETTLED EMOTIONS.

SCORE ONE FOR THE NUDGE

What are the odds that two normally very level-headed people, each over 70 years old, would find themselves falling off their roof? You just can't make this stuff up. What does this have to do with being a nudge? I'll tell you.

I'm a very big believer (as you have read) in having an up-to-date estate plan created by an estate-planning attorney. I'm not fond of situations in which people are their own lawyer via the World Wide Web or they ask their cousin Marty for the name of the attorney who got Marty's kid off a drunk-driving fiasco. I will not ask a divorce attorney to draft documents to take a company public, and I won't ask a mergers and acquisitions attorney to write a prenuptial agreement. I want estate work done by an estate-planning attorney. It's one of the quirks of my personality.

My documents are up-to-date. I feel strongly that all of my clients should have theirs up-to-date as well, particularly clients who are older than me. I have been reminding, ever so gently, two of my clients, who are of the age at which they are now taking required minimum distributions from their IRA account—that's age 70 and a half—that they should be sitting down with an estate-planning attorney because their circumstances have changed dramatically since they had a will created.

Let's call these two fellows Earl and Bernie. Earl is in his mid-70s and has some significant health issues. He and his wife, Roberta, created a will when their kids were in grade school. They now have seven grandchildren from those kids who are all grown and no longer in grade school. They have no documents other than a decades-old will—no health-care directives, no powers of attorney, no trusts, nothing.

Now, to beat the band, Earl thinks of himself as a self-sufficient kind of guy. He doesn't need any help. He climbed up a ladder onto his roof during the winter to clear debris from the gutter. You already know how this ends. It ends badly. The ambulance was in the driveway, taking his badly bruised body to the local hospital just as his wife arrived home from the grocery store. Thankfully, his bruises and ego were the only injuries of the day. It could have been much worse.

I used that occasion to once again be a nudge and remind them that had Earl died from the injuries sustained in the fall, the plans that they had for their kids and the education of their grandkids that they had spoken of might not have come to pass. Two years of pushing and badgering nicely, and nudging, came to a successful conclusion when we agreed that I could assist them in setting up an estate-planning review with a local planning attorney.

It only took Earl falling off the ladder to realize the importance of planning.

Remember I told you that there were two fellows who fell off the roof.

Well, Bernie is quite a character. His stories of growing up in Philadelphia and working in a deli for 40 years never failed to put a smile on my face. His decades of making famous sandwiches helped him to stash away a bundle of cash that found its way into some of the best stocks along with years and years of compounded and reinvested dividends.

You will want to work with your advisor so that you will have enough retirement assets, income, and protection from catastrophic health care events to face your future with confidence.

Their three kids gave them nine grandchildren, and they all live close enough so that Grandpoppy and Grand-mommy can babysit to their hearts' content. Their kids get off easy in that they have free and convenient babysitting services. Sally spends her days playing golf when not with the kids. Bernie plays canasta with the guys and is known to provide a laugh or two on the tennis court.

As the person who had assisted in safeguarding their assets, creating a robust retirement income plan, and crafting their long-term-care policy, I am displeased only with the fact that I have failed to impress upon them the importance of sitting down with an estate-planning attorney. They realize it is important. They know the expense is not a big deal. What they have not been able to get past is that Bernie thinks the kids should get X and Sally thinks the kids should get Y. In other words, they disagree on this, big time.

FORGING BONDS OF STEEL

I've discussed with them the fact that many excellent estate attorneys I know have spent hundreds, if not thousands, of hours in dealing with exactly this kind of difficulty. I would ask them to just spend time with one. I even offered a door-to-door limo service. Well, they could not mentally get to the place where they could take that step, until one fine day—you guessed it—Bernie found himself falling off his roof and breaking his leg.

Obviously, Bernie went up there for a great reason. Of course, he needed no help. Bernie is 72 years old. Sally adores him, but I think she could have killed him for being so stupid. Limping around for several months gave Bernie the time necessary to reconsider his stubborn stance when it came to leaving assets to the kids. I think he was helped along in his thinking by relentless calls from his nudge of an advisor. He and Sally made their way to the attorney. Two months later, they had signed estate-planning documents. Score another one for the nudge.

I recently was chatting with Bernie and Sally in my office, and they talked about that ambulance ride to the hospital. She was by his side but furious. The ambulance driver turned to ask if she was okay, and she said, "No. I'm ready to kill him!" At the hospital, as they wheeled

Bernie inside, the driver kept his hand on the ambulance door and wouldn't let Sally out. "He actually thought I was going to hurt my husband!" Sally told me. ○

BLUEPRINT FOR SUCCESS

"Try not to become a man of success but a man of values."

ALBERT EINSTEIN

M y grandma, Rose, was a girl in her teens when she journeyed from Russia to America. That was long ago, in the early 1900s. Over the many decades and through the many tellings of her story, the details became blurred, such as whether *Bremen* was the name of the ship that bore her to these shores or which German port she had embarked from.

However, one detail stood out sharply for her. She distinctly recalled walking on the deck and looking up at the crow's nest, far above, where a sailor with binoculars was scanning the horizon for icebergs. The ship had struck ice. It was not a disastrous collision like the one that had sliced open the *Titanic*, but the encounter was alarming nonetheless, and the captain had sent a man aloft to alert him to any threats. The ship made it safely to berth in Philadelphia and was moored securely by its great chains, and my grandmother stepped into her new life.

You are the captain of your ship. Your financial advisor sits in the crow's nest, searching the horizon for any threats to your retirement. Your advisor can assist you to steer clear of obstacles in your path and adjust your course to a more prosperous and secure destination.

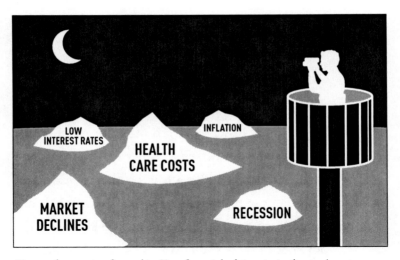

You are the captain of your ship. Your financial advisor sits in the crow's nest, searching the horizon for any threats to your retirement.

EXPECTING THE UNEXPECTED

Sometimes the unexpected happens. Sometimes it happens with a rather big surprise and a large price tag.

Some years ago, a couple with four children were grappling with a problem of providing a college education to each of their kids and still be able to fund their own retirement. It was important to them that their kids graduate college without the burden of student loans. Through a lot of hard work, some innovative financial planning, a great financial advisor, and some very intelligent investments, they will be able to make the goals real.

When one of their kids, the youngest daughter, decided she wanted to become a medical doctor, the family eventually settled upon a plan to make this a reality—again, without the burden of medical school student loans hanging over the head of their youngest child.

Fast forward to a time when the daughter received her degree and began to comply with the usual residency program requirements, affiliating herself with a large teaching hospital in the Southeast. Well, about 18 months into the program, she fell in love with the most wonderful guy she had ever met, and they decided to get married. Within a year of their marriage, she gave birth to twin daughters. To the utter disbelief of her parents, who spent more than $325,000 on her medical education, she never went back into the medical profession. She became a full-time mom.

I was never privy to the family conversations that must have taken place, nor did I even know this family personally. This story was told to me by a friend who practices wealth management in California. But it illustrates a principle that experience has taught many people all too well: everyone has a plan until they're hit in the face.

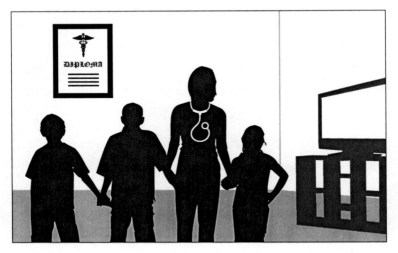

Despite having earned her doctorate, she never practiced and instead raised a family.

I borrowed that phrase, actually, from the world of boxing. Likewise, with your personal financial plan, it is your responsibility to make certain that everything that should be in place is in place. At the time that you or a family member is, as it were, hit in the face, things need to be in place.

The things that may be important in your particular situation may be any number of items, such as a durable power of attorney, a health-care power of attorney, a disability insurance policy, a long-term care insurance policy, life insurance, transfer on death instructions, trusts, personal liability insurance, a family financial and estate-plan organizer notebook, and emergency telephone numbers. That's just a starter list. Work with your attorney and advisor to ensure that they do everything possible to assist you so that your family is prepared.

MY MOTHER PASSED AWAY IN 1969 WHEN I WAS 12 YEARS OLD, PROBABLY 40 YEARS BEFORE HER TIME, FROM BREAST CANCER. BAD THINGS DO HAPPEN TO GOOD PEOPLE.

This is a must before bad things happen. I know from personal and professional experience that bad things happen to good people. My mother passed away in 1969 when I was 12 years old, probably 40 years before her time, from breast cancer. Bad things do happen to good people.

AVOIDING THE UNSCRUPULOUS

And sometimes people do bad things—or make some bad decisions. Imagine the following scenario. Mabel Jones passes away at the age of 67 from congestive heart failure, five years after her husband, Charlie, died from cancer. Their only son, Derek, is 39 and single. Derek works at a bottling plant for one of the major soda companies. He works on the loading dock, driving a forklift, each day shuttling hundreds of pallets full of soda onto waiting tractor trailers. Derek has been dating Jane for eight months. They may or may not be serious. Time will tell.

Derek is informed by his parents' attorney that he is the sole heir to their estate, which consists of his parents' modest home, valued at about $210,000, and some mutual funds that the parents had held for many years. Derek is told that the mutual funds, assorted checking accounts, and a few certificates of deposit total approximately $620,000. Including the house, which he will sell. He will walk away with a cool $800,000 in cash. Derek had no idea his parents had socked away that much money. Derek is ecstatic, as is Jane.

Derek decides to take some upcoming vacation days that he has, and he and Jane jet off to Jamaica for a two-week vacation. They party like there is no tomorrow, spending thousands and thousands of dollars. While there, he meets Rob, who tells him about a surefire options trading program that generates, on average, 50 percent returns per month. Derek, with no investment experience whatsoever, signs up with Rob and his trading program.

Upon returning to New Jersey, Derek sets up the account with Rob's firm and transfers $700,000 into the account. He figures he will keep $75,000 on hand in cash and use the monthly profits to buy some toys. This cannot fail, he figures. Little does he understand what he has gotten himself into, nor with whom he is dealing.

Rob is a trader who has duped unsuspecting people like Derek into signing over all authority on securities accounts while investing in ultra-high-risk trading strategies designed to produce large commissions. Within a short period of time, the money was gone, lost to dubious trading strategies. Derek has also blown the cash that he had kept on the side. He is back at the loading dock, driving his forklift, lamenting on how he blew $800,000 and wondering why Jane won't return his phone calls anymore.

YOUR PRIMER FOR SUCCESS

In this book, I have given you a primer for creating a successful and effective relationship with a financial consultant. Through the use of these ideas and stories, I have provided ample suggestions for you to consider.

The best way for you to ensure a successful ongoing relationship with your advisor is to really think about what you need to accomplish, acknowledge that you must have a plan for its attainment, and communicate those ideas to your advisor. You would not go on vacation without a plan. You would not send your child to a college without planning the type of school, its cost, location, choice of majors, and so on. Sit down and consider what is important for you to accomplish and enlist the aid of your advisor by requesting a meeting to review these ideas.

One of the reasons I have written this book is that I feel the ideas are important to spread. It is my wish that the ideas expressed here will live on for you after you close this book. Make concrete plans to speak with your advisor soon. I hope you have been writing notes in the margins of this book so you can go back and review issues you will want to bring up with your advisor.

What are the *whys* of what you want to accomplish? Do you want to intervene in a meaningful way in your grandchildren's college education funding? Do you want to make sure that family assets are passed on in a particular way? Do you want a significant gift to bypass a generation and go directly to your grandchildren? Would you like to make a significant gift to a college, church, synagogue, or organization? Help your advisor understand the *whys*.

A BROKEN BONE MENDED BECOMES STRONGER

Let me draw an analogy. I have been told that if you break a bone, the area of the break often becomes stronger than it was before the break. I have witnessed breakdowns in client service become the focal point for forging stronger bonds with the client, as mistakes were corrected in a timely manner.

Over the course of your relationship with your financial advisor, something at some time will go wrong. Look at this short list of possible problems, and consider whether any are familiar to you:

misaddressed correspondence *misspelled names*

incorrect data entered into computer *incorrect owner's registrations*

delayed instruction to transfer assets *purchased wrong amount of security*

transfer that was missed *purchased the wrong security*

transfer to the wrong account *call not returned*

The list can go on and on. Where human beings are involved, there is always a chance that a mistake will be made.

What separates superior service from bad service is what happens once the mistake is discovered and known. These are opportunities for your financial advisor and his or her staff to step up, take ownership of the problem, and do everything within their power to make things right as quickly as possible. They must acknowledge that mistakes were made and look to strengthen their processes and procedures so that those mistakes are not repeated.

The character of your advisor will be illuminated by how he or she deals with and solves the problem. If a sincere apology is offered to you in addition to wow service, you have the makings of a closer and stronger bond.

WHEN YOUR ADVISOR IS HAPPIEST

It's all about you. Many times in their careers, advisors see a situation in which they can bring all of their expertise, experience, and resources to bear in support of a client. I call this a wealth-planning home run. It's when we are happiest.

Why? It is when we have done great work that we are proud of. It's when critical items that must be addressed are completed. It is when we shine. It is why we have taken all the tests, attended all the courses and workshops, and read all the books.

It is intellectually challenging to be able to craft an $800,000, $2 million, or $7 million portfolio. It is nice to be able to provide a superior income solution through the use of a particular type of annuity product. But it's entirely different when your advisor can combine the use of many different solutions to solve the highly complex wealth-management issues of a family.

For example, advisors can combine the use of comprehensive financial planning, college savings plans, professionally managed investment portfolios, and life insurance solutions to leverage legacy gifts, and to build customized solutions to complex family issues.

Face it. The more wealth you have, typically, the more complex it is to ensure that your resources are managed properly and for your greatest benefit. I'm not saying that we push complexity. What I am saying is that it's a challenge to do this kind of work, and advisors find it gratifying and rewarding. It is intellectually stimulating.

I consistently ask myself the question, "How could I improve the lives of the clients I serve?" I have made referrals to elder-care specialists and attorneys, estate-planning attorneys, forensic accountants, CPAs, event planners, even root canal specialists and home inspectors. I have purchased books for clients and their kids, given subscriptions to Success Magazine (highly recommended for kids and grandkids) and been a relentless nudge to procrastinators. I have created financial plans, set up educational savings accounts, created lifetime retirement-income streams, and many other things.

I do this because I have a passion for increasing the quality of the lives of the families I serve and to lower the amount of uncertainty in their lives. And that passion is a good match for what my clients consistently tell me they want, which comes down to this: "I want a trusted advisor with decades of experience in working with people like me. I want a financial plan and an investment strategy that I can be comfortable with, that provides me the income I want and the confidence that is important to me."

Would I do it if I did not get paid? Good question. I'm not sure of the answer. Perhaps I could write about that.

WHAT REALLY MATTERS

I knew that operating a laundry was not for me. I remember that I used to be stressed out in college because my dad was, basically, going to leave Norton's laundry to me. Telling him that I didn't want it was one of the most difficult things I ever did. He kept making it better and better for me. That was his plan but not mine.

IT WAS NOT UNTIL YEARS LATER THAT I REALIZED MY MOM, DAD, SHIRLEY, AND MY GRANDMA, ROSE, WORKING WITH ME AT NORTON'S LAUNDRY, HAD HANDED ME THE KEYS OF THE KINGDOM.

It was not until years later that I realized my mom, dad, Shirley, and my grandma, Rose, working with me at Norton's laundry, had handed me the keys of the kingdom. Through their rules and guidance, I developed an unshakable work ethic and grounded myself in these rules.

- Have a clear purpose. Know what you are trying to accomplish.

- There is no room in life for a bad attitude or poor performance.

- Be honest with yourself and others.

- You will make mistakes, but what is important is to use them as lessons and to learn from them.

- You will succeed by helping and serving others.

- Keep improving your skills and knowledge.

- Always listen carefully before speaking.

This set of rules and this clear focus have become my mental blueprint. That has been the true legacy that my family left to me, and it is my privilege to share it with my clients and with you, the reader. Sound investments certainly can generate wealth, but what truly enriches us is the quality of our relationships.

SOUND INVESTMENTS CERTAINLY CAN GENERATE WEALTH, BUT WHAT TRULY ENRICHES US IS THE QUALITY OF OUR RELATIONSHIPS.

I wish you a long, happy, and prosperous life.

CPSIA information can be obtained at www.ICGtesting.com
Printed in the USA
BVOW03s1815110714

358708BV00004B/14/P

EX LIBRIS

UNIVERSITATIS SANCTI JOANNIS